Muriel Ck

The Banquet:

My Grandma's Memories of China

Emily Foster

iUniverse, Inc.
New York   Bloomington

The Banquet

My Grandma's Memories of China

Copyright © 2008 by Emily Foster

All rights reserved. No part of this book may be used or reproduced by any means, graphic, electronic, or mechanical, including photocopying, recording, taping or by any information storage retrieval system without the written permission of the publisher except in the case of brief quotations embodied in critical articles and reviews.

The views expressed in this work are solely those of the author and do not necessarily reflect the views of the publisher, and the publisher hereby disclaims any responsibility for them.

iUniverse books may be ordered through booksellers or by contacting:

iUniverse
1663 Liberty Drive
Bloomington, IN 47403
www.iuniverse.com
1-800-Authors (1-800-288-4677)

Because of the dynamic nature of the Internet, any Web addresses or links contained in this book may have changed since publication and may no longer be valid. The views expressed in this work are solely those of the author and do not necessarily reflect the views of the publisher, and the publisher hereby disclaims any responsibility for them.

ISBN: 978-0-595-52957-5 (pbk)
ISBN: 978-1-4401-0797-9 (cloth)
ISBN: 978-0-595-63010-3(ebk)

Printed in the United States of America

iUniverse rev. date: 12/12/2008

Author's Note

I have chosen to use the old spelling of 'Chengtu' and 'Szechuan'; the way they were spelled when Grandma lived there. In recent years, the spelling has become more phonetic, and so you may see variations such as Chengdu, and Sichuan.

This book is based on my grandmother's memories of China from 1922 until 1968. I also relied on 45 year-old tape recordings of my great-grandfather telling stories about his escape to Hong Kong.

Acknowledgments:

I owe many thanks to the countless people who helped me with this project along the way. Some of you gave me ideas, some told me your stories, took time and energy reading my manuscript and offering your suggestions, and some cheered me on from the sidelines. I'd like to acknowledge the following people for being essential to *The Banquet*'s completion: Kendall and Judy Anderson, Catherine Foster, Susan Chambers, Olaf Kitchen, Auntie Lydia, Aunt Gwen, Snow and Susie, Gary, Mr. Li, my friends at Chengdu Daily, the friendly staff at People's Hospital Number Two, Qi YaNan, Pat Tonge, Joe Grigg, Matthew Swan, Anna Kim, Jaye Blakely, Jean Weese, my agent Peter Taylor, Mom, Dad, and to my uncle Murray, who took me aside years ago and stressed the importance of completing a book like this one.

I dedicate this book to the Tonge family, and to all the loving, dedicated, storytelling grandmas out there. Especially mine.

Contents

1. February 2006 – Is Your Grandmother Chinese? 1
2. Growing up in Chengtu – 1920's 7
3. Beautiful Yangshuo – 2006 20
4. Treacherous Trip Home – 1947 24
5. A Western Housewife 39
6. Exiled 48
7. Escaping Like a Criminal 62
8. A Granddaughter's Quest 73
9. Hong Kong Stories 81
10. Grandma's Umbrella 116
11. From Babies to Opium Addicts 118
12. Leaving again for the Last Time 127
13. The Beginning 130

Introduction:

On February 9th, 2006, following in the footsteps of my great-grandmother Beatrice Kitchen, my grandmother Muriel Tonge, and my mother Leslie Foster, I packed my bags, said goodbye to family and friends in Toronto, and boarded a plane for China.

As a child in Grandma's lap I'd listened to stories about a vibrant people in a mysterious country on the other side of the world. With her incredible memory, my grandmother lit my imagination with the joys of West China, where she had spent her childhood.

When I grew old enough to appreciate her endless exotic anecdotes, romantic and terrifying adventures, the dream of my own journey began to emerge.

My great-grandparents, John and Beatrice Kitchen, left their home in Griffin, Saskatchewan to work in China in 1920. John had accepted a position as superintendent of a Christian printing house in Chengtu, the capital of Szechuan province. Here, Beatrice would apply her artistic talent and training in the production of illustrations for the church's literature, pamphlets and brochures.

My grandmother's stories move easily and naturally into her own life growing up with her sisters, Christine and Gwen, within the protective walls of the mission compound for the first 16 years of her life. In her late teens my grandmother returned to Canada where, after completing her nursing degree at the University of Saskatoon, she married my grandfather, Walton Tonge.

For Walton—another resident of Griffin—my grandmother's parents and the stories they told while visiting Griffin on leave from their missionary work had inspired his entering the ministry, and travelling abroad. For my grandmother, the return to China was the beginning of a life providing help to people in need, giving comfort to those needing comfort, tending to medical problems and sharing in the day-to-day lives of her Chinese community.

Together, the handsome young preacher and his nurse bride left Canada for the Orient in 1947, two years beyond the end of World

War II. After two weeks in their new home, my mother, Leslie Tonge, was born—the third generation to live in China.

*

At the urging of others, my grandmother made several attempts at putting her China life on paper. Although she still gives frequent presentations on her work in China, she soon grew wearied and frustrated at not finding the right words for her memoir. Without thinking about what I was getting myself into, I stepped up and offered to take on the task. I knew, as much as anyone who heard her stories, that someone needed to write them down. I love to write. Why not me?

In the fall of 2004, my 82-year-old grandmother, her four adult children and my father ventured to Hong Kong to revisit friends and their old home. While work prevented me from accompanying them, their stories, photographs and videos convinced me that I too was destined to visit and explore China.

Where my grandmother's stories had once been entertaining glimpses into another time, they suddenly became an inspiration to me, and I found myself plying her for more details about her life there. I began reading every book I could find about that sprawling giant of a country across the world—political and cultural histories, travel books, biographies of famous and infamous Chinese personalities.

In the fall of 2005 I accepted a position as a teacher at an English college in Yangshuo, a small town (by Chinese standards) of 30,000 people in the gorgeous province of Yangshuo. Although my grandmother was far away in Canada, I kept her stories and words of wisdom close by.

She still loves to quote Churchill who said, "We make a living by what we get, but we make a life by what we give."

And Einstein, who said, "Great spirits have always encountered violent opposition from mediocre minds."

Then there's a saying she loves from an unknown philosopher: "God gave each man two ends ... one to think with and one to sit on. Man's success depends on the end he uses most."

Grandma Tonge has spent her whole life serving others, both in China and Canada. After she and Walton left Hong Kong for good in

1968, she worked for Scarborough Public Health as a nurse, in schools, in hospitals, and in local clinics. She has been awarded the *Anson Taylor Award* for outstanding education in Scarborough Ontario. She also received the *Scarborough Bicentennial Civic Award of Merit* for her excellence in the area of Public Health.

Muriel Tonge has touched and inspired people all over the world, and will continue to do so for many, many years to come.

Grandma has always wanted us, her grandchildren, to take her many stories, sayings, and inspirational quotes to heart, by enriching our lives by doing things for other people. She loves to remind us, in a firm but friendly tone, "Whatever you do, don't starve at the banquet!"

The journey that led me to mingle my China stories with hers has brought me to a place where I can truly appreciate what she means.

*

Chapter 1

Is Your Grandmother Chinese?

February 2006

    In China, whenever I told people I was Canadian, they always said, "Just like Dr. Norman Bethune!"
    One morning I decided to ask my students at the English Language College in Yangshuo why this particular Canadian is so famous in their country.
    One student, who'd chosen "Saint" for his English name, told me that in Chinese society they like to choose one person to emulate. They "chose" Dr. Bethune because he was a Western man who had lived there for many years and helped to bring medical advances to the Chinese people. Eventually he died in China, becoming even more of a hero.
    Another student, with the English name Stephanie, told me that Chairman Mao had written about Bethune, praising him for his bravery and for his contributions to China and the Chinese people. Since then, Chinese students throughout this giant country read about Dr. Bethune in school textbooks.
    All eight students in this English class were well educated, and in their mid to late twenties. I asked them if they knew of any other foreigners who had lived and worked in China, people who left their home countries to help the Chinese people by starting schools, universities, hospitals, or by working as doctors, nurses, teachers and dentists. They shook their heads.
    Tossing my English lesson aside, I leaned forward in my chair and told them that my great-grandparents had moved to China in 1920. My grandmother and mother had both been born in China. Believe it

or not I am the fourth generation of women on my mother's side who has lived and worked here!"

They stared at me, agape, until finally I saw a hand raised at the back of the classroom. It was Grant, with his large confident grin. "Is your grandmother Chinese?" he asked.

I smiled, shaking my head. "My great-grandmother, a Canadian, died here, and my great-grandfather, also Canadian, lived in Chengtu for 31 years. For him, Chengtu was his hometown," I explained. "Hometown" is a word that carries a lot of weight in China. My students nodded their approval.

After navigating them through my family tree on the whiteboard at the front of the classroom, I launched into the stories of my grandmother's experiences in China as a child, and later as a nurse and mother. When I realized that we had run into noon hour, I suggested breaking for lunch, but no one showed any interest in moving. I hadn't seen a single student glance up at the clock for over an hour.

They had never heard personal stories about a foreigner in China in the 1920's and 30's. The idea that my grandmother, a Canadian, had grown up in a Chinese city, and had returned to China after finishing university in Canada, amazed them. They had only ever known about Bethune, and his work with the Chinese in their fight against the Japanese.

After the students filed out of the classroom, I looked down at my book of lesson plans and thought about setting them aside and telling the rest of my classes about Grandma Tonge. They sloved to hear anything from our personal lives. And truthfully, I never grew tired of telling her stories.

Muriel Kitchen, was born in West China, and grew up within the brick-walled confines of a missionary compound. On the other side of the walls, Chengtu streets clamoured with bicycles, merchants, markets, and stray dogs. Since the turn of the century, missionaries in China had lived in compounds to be somewhat protected from foreign diseases, since vaccines weren't readily available at the time. The thick walls also ensured privacy and protection from robbers. Foreigners always attracted large crowds of curious Chinese onlookers, so it was hard to get a moment's peace without retreating behind high walls.

Missionaries at the turn of the 20th century came from all denominations of the Christian Church to offer new ideas to the Chinese people. Just as some people today seek answers in different teachings and philosophies, many Chinese at the turn of the century turned to the foreign missionaries for something new and hopeful.

For thousands of years, China had been ruled again and again by haughty Emperors. Dynasties came and went, changing the shape and history of the country. The last Dynasty, the Qing, was renowned for being especially weak and corrupt, caving to the demands of pushy foreign groups who sailed into Chinese ports demanding trade. As the 19th century came to a close, the Chinese people grew more and more weary of their country's leaders. As the Qing continued to give pieces of their country away, (Hong Kong to the British, Macau to the Portuguese, Taiwan to the Japanese), the rumblings of a revolution grew louder. The voice behind the rumblings was an American-educated man, Dr. Sun Yat-sen, who eventually became known as the father of new China. Through his work with revolutionaries, including Chiang Kai-shek, Dr. Sun eventually contributed to the Emperor's removal from office, and successfully crumbled the Chinese Dynasty tradition in 1911.

The Kitchens were one of six families living in the Canadian missionary compound in the 1920s. Each family lived in a spacious, three-storey brick house surrounded by colourful flower and vegetable gardens. It was a sheltered but active place, with both people and critters. Malaria-carrying mosquitoes drove people behind ghostly nets at night; snakes sometimes wiggled their way into beds, and owls hooted from rafters all around.

Muriel's compound had one large gate at either end, which was guarded by a gateman who was in charge of who came and went. If any of the missionaries needed a rickshaw, he would hail one and negotiate the price.

The missionary families hired cooks and servants called "amahs," which was common practice. It was frowned upon if foreigners didn't provide jobs for local Chinese people. Amahs took care of the children and helped with the housework, while the cooks either prepared all the meals, or assisted the missionary wives with shopping and meals. The Kitchen family had an amah named Lin Da Neung who helped to manage the household while John and Beatrice worked.

Beside the collection of missionary houses stood the Canadian Mission Press, which printed and distributed Christian pamphlets, newsletters, Sunday school lessons, and bibles throughout West China.

John Kitchen, Muriel's father, was the superintendent, responsible for one hundred employees.

Beatrice, Muriel's mother, illustrated Bible stories using rice paper, which was then turned upside down onto a block of wood. A team of carvers would then carve out the negative in order to make and distribute thousands of lively ink prints. Her drawings depicted Chinese people as the well-known Biblical characters. She was known to go out into the cramped streets of Chengtu to study the people and their surroundings. The resulting prints were rich in detail and Chinese character. It wasn't long before the men and women of the marketplaces knew Mrs. Kitchen as a gentle lady, with a keen interest in China and its people.

Some examples of ink block prints by Beatrice Kitchen.

A sketch by Beatrice Kitchen.

*

When I was a child, Grandma spoke about China so often that her stories didn't register as exciting or exotic. Being children, we had other things we wanted to do besides listening to anecdotes about starving orphans and rickshaw rides.

It wasn't until I was a university student (I hate to admit) when I started really listening to my grandmother's stories.

A group of my friends were discussing grandparents and family history when I casually mentioned that my Grandma Tonge had been born in China.

"What??? Is she Chinese?"

It was an honest mistake, even though I look about as Chinese as a peanut butter sandwich. The name "Tonge" (which, I've been told, may actually be French, from the name de Tonge), does sound like the Chinese name Tong, so I forgave the assumption.

I was very embarrassed when I couldn't answer the landslide of questions that followed. I didn't know if Grandma had been in China when the Communists took over, and I wasn't sure exactly what she did in Hong Kong, except that it had to do with abandoned babies.

The next time I saw Grandma, I paid attention when she started into one of her stories. While my other family members mumbled among themselves (they'd heard Grandma's stories so many times, they knew the build-up, punch-line and moral of every one of them), I leaned in a little closer.

The more questions I asked, the more fascinating her stories became, and the more I realized that I hardly knew my grandmother at all.

The first thing I needed to do was go back to the beginning, to find out how my family ended up in China in the first place.

Chapter 2

Growing up in Chengtu – 1920's

"Do you mind if I tape record this, Grandma?"
"Not at all, honey. Should I speak slowly?"
"No, that's okay."
"Have some more of your sandwich."

Dad—John Kitchen—and his brother William were born in Porthleven, a tiny English fishing village, in 1894 and 1896. Their father, a fisherman, could not afford to send his sons to university, so Dad became a printer and lay minister in the Methodist church. Uncle Willy became a cobbler.

In 1913, when he was nineteen, Dad came to Canada, looking for adventure. While he was studying to become a minister in Griffin, Saskatchewan, he met and fell in love with a quiet, well-mannered girl named Beatrice McDowell.

When World War One broke out, he left Canada to fight in Europe. He refused to carry or shoot a rifle, so instead he carried a stretcher in the front lines in the medical corps. He also carried a picture of my mother in his breast pocket. They got married shortly after he returned from the war.

My mother worked as an artist for the Eaton's department store catalogue division. Although she drew sketches of elegant dresses, hats and shoes, she didn't care much for fashion. A dress was a dress. As a young woman, she refused to wear a bra or corset because she thought it spoiled the natural lines of one's body. Dad was drawn to her quiet kindness. She wasn't the type to light up a room, but her presence was always warm and comforting.

Dad finished his minister's training right around the time the Methodist Church was appealing for new missionaries for their centre in West China. As luck would have it, they were calling for a printer, an artist and ministers. Obviously my parents were ideal candidates, and it so happened that both felt a pull to work overseas, in a country in which they felt their help was needed. So, a short time later, my parents and their first baby, Christine, were on their way to start a new life in West China. It was 1920.

My parents learned to speak Mandarin in the small town of Juenhsien (*Yoo-in-shan*). After their first two years in China they had their second daughter, Muriel; me. A short time after I was born we moved to Chengtu, the capital of Szechuan province, where Dad was going to work as the superintendent of the Canadian Mission Press.

In 1924, my younger sister Gwen was born. The three of us, Christine, myself, and Gwen, became known around the compound as the "Kitchenettes."

Three Kitchen girls, Muriel, Gwen and Christine. 1932. Photo by John Kitchen

Birthday Kites. 1932. Photo by John Kitchen.

As young children growing up in China we didn't have any toys, radios or televisions to entertain us. We climbed trees, made dolls out of old rags, played house with the other missionary children and had a few kites. My birthday falls in March, as does my sister Gwen's. Since March was the best kite-flying month, we were usually given kites as birthday presents. The year I turned ten we got two colourful butterfly kites that were as tall as we were. We considered ourselves to be expert flyers, so we would let our kites fly up and over the compound wall until they were tiny specks in the air, like fleas on a pillow of cloud. If other kids were flying kites, we would challenge them to have "kite fights," which involved steering our kites over theirs, in order to control both kites with one string. If we pulled hard enough, we could cut an opponent's string, and they would lose their kite and have to go running after it.

On the other side of the north wall of our compound was a large field used by warlord armies for drills. One windy day, after having an exciting kite-fight with anonymous kite-flyers on the other side of the wall, and retrieving a large, black, dragon-shaped kite, we heard a loud banging at the gates. Dad left his office at the printing press to investigate the racket. He found a pack of red-faced Chinese soldiers standing outside, demanding the return of their kite! "What seems to be the problem?" he asked them.

"Our kite has been stolen by someone from this compound. It disappeared over your wall," one of the soldiers barked.

"Dear me," said Dad, scratching his head. "Let me take a look."

Sure enough he found their black kite tangled up with our butterfly kites, abandoned in a heap near the front gate.

By this time Gwen and I were trembling under our beds. Dad returned the kite, apologized for the inconvenience, and peace was restored.

Our compound was about three miles from the Canadian school, which was located outside the city walls, next to the Chinese university, (which is now Szechuan University). The Canadian School was a boarding and day school for missionary children from all over West China, and from all denominations of the Christian church. Our teachers were missionary teachers from Canada. My sisters and I were part of the few who boarded from Monday to Friday, but went home to the compound for weekends.

At school we were kept busy with sports, Scouts, plays, field trips to historic sites, French classes, and lessons in etiquette and decorum. I regret that as children we were never taught Mandarin at school. We picked up bits and pieces of the local street slang, but were never taught at school how to converse properly. Since we were sheltered at home and attended an English-language school, we didn't have enough exposure to proper Mandarin to become fluent as children.

The Canadian school was a large, three-story brick building, covered in dark curtains of ivy. There was electricity but no running water, so warm water had to be delivered by servants to our door each morning in small tubs so that we could wash ourselves.

The toilets, as in all the homes, were toilet seats perched over a pail. Farmers collected the full pails (affectionately known as "honey buckets") for fertilizer. This was, and still is why eating raw vegetables is a problem in China. All of us had worms at one point or other because of the vegetables being fertilized with human feces. I was a very wormy child because my favourite food was Chinese pickles, which were notoriously unclean. My sisters and I had to take de-worming medicine every six months.

A busy street in Chengtu, seen from atop the city wall. Photo by John Kitchen.

On Fridays after school the central walk from the gatehouse would be lined with rickshaws, ready for those of us who went home for the weekend. The three-mile ride back to the compound led us along cramped, noisy streets. Some of the older students would ride their bicycles to school, running the risk of bumping into rickshaws, other bicycles, or worse, the full honey buckets on the side of the road waiting to be collected by farmers.

My sisters and I had one outfit for the whole week and one pair of shoes for the whole year. Naturally, with all the running around we did, our shoes got so tattered by the end of the year that our toes poked out of the thin fabric, and the soles shrunk to thin wafers.

We grew up in far from affluent circumstances, but were surrounded by others who had even less than we did. Mother was always bringing peasant mothers and their babies into our home to give them a good meal and a bath. I remember watching her show one wide-eyed mother how to properly clean an infant so that it wouldn't die of infections. Our baby clothes were given away, along with whatever else we had outgrown. Mother was always making baby clothes for children in need.

I remember going to the marketplace and seeing beggar children lining the streets selling woven baskets. The children were bent and deformed so people would pity them and give money. I was told that some of their parents were so poor that they deformed their own children on purpose to try and earn more money. Many of the children in the marketplace, my age or younger, had twisted spines, or missing limbs. Their eyes were large and sunken. Their translucent skin clung to their skeletal bodies like wet paper, and was covered in dark bruises and smudges of dirt. It was a mystery to me how anyone could walk past them without digging around for a coin or two. After every trip to the market, I became increasingly aware that there was a lot of sadness and pain in the world.

Summers were hot in Chengtu so many missionary families would escape to the mountain villages where it was cooler. Together, a large pack of us would travel by sedan chair (an enclosed chair resting on long boards, carried by two men on foot) and rickshaw out of the city, into the surrounding mountains. It would usually take a day or two of travelling.

Several times we would stop for snacks along the way, much as you would during any family trip, and the local farmers would gather around to watch our every move. I remember stopping in one small village and pulling out our bundled lunches, which included multiple tins of food. The locals gasped collectively in delight as they watched my mother open the tins. It must have seemed magical to them, seeing a small metal container with a picture of carrots on the outside, opened up to reveal bright orange carrot sticks inside. Next there was a can with a picture of peaches on the outside. The can with the picture of peas contained peas. Well, imagine their shock and disgust when one of the young missionary mothers pulled out a tin of baby food with a picture of a baby on the outside! Oh, the horror! The rural folks yelped and ran away from us without looking back!

The families from our compound would go to Juanhsien, where we lived in flimsy one-room shacks without running water or electricity. We fetched our drinking water from a nearby mountain stream. Narrow paths laced through forests of slender bamboo surrounding our little cabin. Further down the mountain were terraced fields, and miles upon miles of watery rice paddies.

To pass the time, my sisters and I sometimes played in the Buddhist temples, where we would climb the larger-than-life idols guarding the entrance. We would sneak off with the sticks of burning incense to use as magic wands.

One day, one of my friends claimed to have seen a wild boar grunting and sniffing around behind her cottage. Our parents had previously told us that wild boars were known to be dangerous if provoked. I'd heard they could be downright nasty, charging at you with their ugly tusks. To quench our curiosity five of us decided to venture out in search of wild boars up the mountainside. Off we went, a troupe of fierce children, armed with nothing but sticks and determination.

Not far into the thick of the forest, after abandoning the trail, we heard huffing and grunting behind some bushes. We froze, our hearts hammering. At the snap of a twig, we tore through the trees and scampered down the hill, hollering and wailing, branches and bushes scratching at our bare legs.

Minutes later we came across a large cornfield plateau that had been cut into the mountainside. The farmers looked up from their work and saw six kids tearing out of the woods, pushing the towering stalks of corn aside. The farmers shouted and chased us, waving their sickles above their heads.

Thankfully, we were fast and outran them. My sisters and I sprinted all the way home and dove under our beds. Mother came into the house and smirked down at us. "Now what have you done?"

That was the last boar hunt for all of us. To this day I'm not sure if the grunting we heard was really a boar, or our imaginations running wonderfully wild.

One year, we were forced to evacuate to a small mission station in the mountains. I was ten, and the warlord battles in Chengtu, the largest city in West China, had grown violent. Often warlord armies would battle over territories. My sisters and I had grown up with constant conflict exploding on the other side of the compound wall. Slowly the battle sounds came closer until one day we were playing outside the house in a fort we had built when we heard the sharp clatter of gunfire in the distant fields. We glanced up at each other, and continued calmly playing. Our father was red in the face when he raced to pull us inside the house, away from our fort. A short time later we discovered a stray bullet lodged in my sister Christine's bed! Dad had us sleep on the floor pressed up against the wall after that.

We eventually evacuated to Renshow, a mountain town to the north of Chengtu. There were five missionary families crammed together in two houses for a period of several months, while the warlord armies fought over Chengtu. Our mothers taught the school lessons.

Having pets helped keep us occupied. My sisters liked to look after goats and rabbits. I liked ducklings. Loolie Wibblewobble was part of a family of six abandoned ducklings that we found by a nearby stream. Wildcats had come down from the hills at night, and taken the ducklings one by one until only Loolie Wibblewobble was left.

Ducks are loyal, friendly, and ever so affectionate as pets. Their lack of toilet training was the only problem I can recall. Once my sisters and I tried fashioning a cloth diaper for Loolie, but it wouldn't stay on, and only ended up making more of a mess. We had trouble keeping up with his accidents, much to the dismay of our amah, Lin Da Neung. She ran around cleaning up the copious messes. Wonderful woman. She was so patient with us.

Loolie Wibblewobble was a very timid little duck, so he became quite attached to me. He followed me everywhere, and even sat in my lap during prayer meetings (when groups of missionaries would get together for an hour each week to sit in a circle and pray).

One day I took a troupe of friends up into the hills behind our cottage to try and catch the rotten wildcat that had eaten Loolie's family. I brandished a large stick, ready to attack anything that moved. I beat at the bushes, and threw stones into the caves where wildcats were said to sleep. Minutes after our ascent up the hill, we heard shouting from down below. It was a large group of angry mothers.

"Come back here, children!"

"What are you thinking, disappearing up there?"

"It's dangerous!"

With shoulders slumped, we trudged back down the hill.

As it turned out, a wildcat wouldn't be Loolie's demise. One sunny day, my friends and I were running down a trail towards a stream at the bottom of the hill. Loolie's little webbed feet just couldn't keep up with us. He waddled and flapped, but got in the way of one young boy, whose legs were flying down the stone steps faster than he thought possible. The boy lost control, and his foot came crashing down on Loolie's head, killing him instantly. Poor little duck.

In 1937, Nationalists were fighting Communists in cities all over the country, and both were trying to fend off the Japanese armies who wanted to overthrow the major cities in China.

Every seven years, missionaries were granted a year-long furlough to go back to their home countries to visit their families. In 1937 my parents knew it was a good time for us to leave. I was fifteen, and was too preoccupied with the exciting trip we were about to take to worry about China's political situation. The last time I'd left China, I was 8, so my memory of Canada was foggy, but I was still excited about the trip.

The journey home required riverboats, trains, planes and lots of stops in between. My parents decided to take the opportunity to travel a little on our way to Canada that year.

After several train and boat rides, we arrived in Shanghai, where I saw posters advertising Palmolive soap. Supposedly, Palmolive gave you beautiful skin, and like any fifteen-year-old girl, I wanted beautiful skin more than anything. So I took my hard-earned allowance and bought a smooth, green bar of soap. It was easy to save up my allowance (a dollar per month) because in Chengtu there wasn't anything I ever wanted to buy. Palmolive soap was the first thing I'd ever purchased for myself. I remember holding the bar under my nose and breathing in the wonderful soapy smell. During our travels, everyone in my family kept borrowing it so by the time we got home there was nothing left except a thin little rectangle.

Next, we took a boat from Shanghai to Manchuria, where we then boarded the Trans-Siberian railway. The church had provided Dad with second-class tickets for our family, which he traded for fifth-class tickets so that we had some extra travel money. This meant that we missed out on second-class luxuries such as cushioned seats (our seats in fifth-class were just wooden benches) and available hot water.

I remember watching the Japanese soldiers boarding the train after us with long black guns slung over their shoulders. At the time I didn't understand what they were doing going to Russia, or why they acted fierce all the time, pacing up and down the train. My sisters and I had no idea that a major world war was about to break out, and the Japanese armies were attempting to conquer China from all sides. The soldiers scowled and pulled the blinds down, threatening to throw everyone off if anyone was caught looking out the windows. Any time the soldiers' backs were turned, my sisters and I would take a peak outside, trying to catch a glimpse of what they didn't want us to see. There were no gardens, no colours, and no happy people waving at the train as we rumbled by. Just flat, cold stretches of barren Siberian landscape. My sisters and I couldn't figure out what all the fuss was about.

Our cabins on the train had four rickety metal bunks. Gwen and I slept above Dad and Mum. Because Christine was the oldest, she had to sleep with three strangers in a different cabin.

The top bunks didn't have any guardrails, so one night I turned over in my sleep and rolled right off the mattress and fell off the bunk. Fast as a blink, my mother sat up, held out her arms and caught me before I could crash to the floor. She picked me up, smoothed back my hair, and tucked me into bed once more. The speed of her reaction didn't even puzzle me back then. (From then on, my parents strapped a belt over my bunk to keep me from falling out. Moving down to the safer bottom bunk wasn't an option because for some reason my parents insisted on sleeping closer to the ground.)

Each time the train stopped at a station, my dad made my sisters and me run up and down the platform for exercise. It was also our job to fill pails with hot water to warm up tins of food for our dinner. While running around off the train, we had to have eyes in the backs of our heads because the train could get moving at any time. We didn't get any warning whistles, or cries of "All aboard!" so people got left behind all the time.

Once we almost lost Mother in a herd of people boarding the train. Father held onto us, his fingers digging into my soft upper arm, while he frantically scanned the crowd. "She was right behind me a second ago," he grumbled. My sister Christine suddenly pointed and cried, "There she is!" Mother was standing with a young couple a few cars down, holding and comforting their screaming infant. Dad's grip on my arm relaxed.

Over the course of the two-week train ride, we passed the time with card games, storytelling, eating tinned food, and occasionally peeking out the window at the desolate Russian landscape.

We visited Moscow, where my sisters and I were given pins bearing the hammer and sickle—the symbol of communism. Dad promptly made us remove the pins from our jackets, telling us that he didn't want didn't want us connected to anything political.

Next we travelled through Poland and Germany, where we took a bus tour that stopped in front of Adolf Hitler's house. We were told by the tour guide not to mention his name. Not even in a whisper.

Finally, we visited my father's family in Porthleven, a small fishing village on the west coast of England. Life there was very different from what we were used to. In China we had been free to entertain ourselves in our spare time. In England we found ourselves bound by many stiff rules. Sundays in Porthleven were for going to church—twice. There would be no swimming, no playing or reading anything but the Bible. My sisters and I got into trouble with our English aunt once because she'd seen us speaking to a girl who was wearing lipstick! Well, good heavenly days! We had been brought up to accept all people for who they were, not for what they look like, nor whether they wore lipstick or read novels on Sundays. Dad eventually got tired of coming to our defense with his relatives, so he told us to stop being so friendly to strangers all the time. We were guests, and had to consider the feelings of our hosts.

The Banquet

We left England by ship at the end of August, and were back in Griffin, Saskatchewan in time to start a fresh school year.

In those days, Griffin was a tiny farm town with a population of about three hundred. One of my first memories of Griffin was my Grade One class at school, back when we were on furlough in 1928. One of the town boys, Walton Tonge, sat across the aisle from me, and was a regular pain in the neck. He did naughty things like putting clumps of mud under my desk so I'd get in trouble from our teacher for not wiping off my boots properly.

After sixteen years in China, and following our trip on the Trans-Siberian railway, I was in grade eleven. Walton Tonge once again had his desk across from mine. This time he was a little friendlier. So were many of the teenage boys in Griffin. Three new teenage girls arriving in Griffin was a big deal in a town of three hundred and Walton Tonge was the catch of the class as far as all the girls were concerned. He was tall, blond, and as gentle as they come.

My sisters, parents and I lived on my uncle Estey's farm. He had his own family, so the house was pretty cramped while we were there, especially since my two cousins were teenage girls as well. We took up a lot of space, especially with the boys who came to visit on a regular basis. Poor Dad was a nervous wreck. His daughters had little or no experience with farm boys. Uncle Estey sent us out to the fields with wagons and pitchforks, telling us to fill the wagons with hay. "That will keep 'em busy," he told my Dad. "Busy girls don't have time to socialize."

Well, the local farm boys came, took our pitchforks out of our hands and chatted to us while they completed all of our work, much to my father's chagrin.

Walton told me many years later that the boys of Griffin had an understanding about the Kitchen girls. Apparently we were "off limits."

When it came to living like the other teenagers in rural Canada, we three were clueless. Growing up in our missionary bubble with the same group of wholesome friends had sheltered us from learning many truths. Any of the boys could have easily taken advantage of us; we were that naïve.

When our furlough ended in 1938, it was decided that Christine and I would stay in Canada to continue our schooling while Gwen, Dad and Mother returned to West China. It would be another seven years before I would see either of my parents again. Seven years, with only telegrams and letters to keep in touch! It was very difficult to say goodbye to them when the time came. Father told Christine and me over and over that this was the way of the missionary life—the way it had to be. No matter how he and mother tried to justify it, I was heartbroken.

Christine and I had some very lonely years after that, particularly around the holidays, and especially because of the war overseas. We were worried sick about our parents and younger sister, who were right in the middle of it. Chengtu was under constant threat of Japanese takeover, as it was the largest city in West China. Years later I heard one story about a particular bomb raid when father gathered everyone from the printing press into an underground bomb shelter, then noticed that my mother was missing. Through the smoke and dust he ran up to her studio, where she worked on her wood block prints. There he found her at her desk, bent over a sketch as another bomb screamed by in the distance. "What are you doing?" Dad hollered.

Mother calmly replied, "If it's my time to die, then I'd rather get killed instantly by a bomb up here, than be smothered and die slowly down there in the bunker. Besides, I'm behind in my work. I need to get this done."

Thankfully, the raid was over only moments later, so Dad didn't have to resort to dragging her to the shelter.

Letters from our parents with such stories came once a month, but it was never enough. They spared us the details (about Chengtu being bombed frequently by the Japanese) but we knew they were in great danger. Not being informed of their situation was the worst part. Having to concentrate on my studies while worrying about whether or not my family was still alive was a nightmare. Thankfully I made some good friends at school, who were very understanding, and who didn't mind if I cried on their shoulders once in a while.

After two years away, Gwen joined Christine and me in Saskatchewan to start her years at university. It was a great relief to see her again, safe and sound, and with news from our parents that everything was okay for them in Chengtu.

Christine took the separation from our parents particularly hard. She worked hard at school as well, studying to become a nurse, but found the transition difficult. Moving from our sheltered life in Chengtu, to a rural life in Canada without our parents was especially tough on Christine. My gentle older sister was vulnerable, with very few defenses of her own, and sometime in her late teens she began to look at the world differently than I did. She met people with strong ideas about Christian faith, and soon began to take solace in those ideas. As the years went by, while at university, Christine became extremely religious, to the extent that she felt that even dancing was a sin, as was eating sugar, wearing anything but 100% pure wool or cotton, and drinking alcohol, even on special occasions.

Back then there were people known as called "missionary casualties," who were children of missionary families who broke under the pressures and the demands of missionary life: living in a foreign country, adjusting between cultures, and constantly being separated from the ones you love. It was too much for some young hearts and minds. Many turned to drugs or alcohol, including some of the missionary children I grew up with in Chengtu. If you ask me, some people spent too much time concentrating on helping others in the mission, and not enough spent taking care of themselves and their families. Many missionary casualties were too fragile at heart to cope. Some, like my sister Christine, turned to extreme forms of religion to feel a sense of belonging. We were grateful that it was religion, and not alcohol or drugs, but after her university years Christine was never the same again. We lost her to her rigid ideas about purity and sin.

Walton Tonge and I became close during that lonely year after my parents left, and while Christine was at university. Many other boys from Griffin were leaving to join the army, but Walton wanted to go to the University of Toronto to become a minister. I was going to follow Christine's footsteps and go to University of Saskatoon to study nursing. After Walton and I left Griffin, we wrote letters back and forth throughout university. We saw each other as often as we could over various holiday visits to Griffin. Before I knew it, the boy who sat across the aisle from me in school had become my sweetheart.

And I began a new chapter of my life.

*

Chapter 3

Beautiful Yangshuo

2006

While playing with the idea of teaching English in China, I knew I didn't want a job in Chengtu. Although it was the city of Grandma Tonge's youth, and was also the place where my mother had been born, I didn't want to live in a large industrial city. I'd read and heard many recent stories from English teachers about respiratory problems and infections from air pollution, and wanted to find a cleaner place in which to live.

I found all sorts of information online about a town in the southern province of Guangxi called Yangshuo. I read that Yangshuo was treasured as one of the most beautiful regions in China. After browsing through pictures, I was instantly intrigued by the green, hump-like mountains—enormous camel backs poking up across the landscape. Instead of cutting into the steep slopes by blasting through the rocks, Yangshuo had developed amid the mountains. The town's homes, roads and shops filled the narrow spaces between and around the humps, spreading right to the bases of every mountain, and up to the edge of the winding Li River. With a manageable population of about 30 000, most of them living in the expansive countryside surrounding Yangshuo proper, I felt deep in my gut that this was the place for me. Clean air, friendly people, an array of opportunities for outdoor activities, and to top it off, job openings for English teachers!

Grandma's eyes sparkled when I told her about my plan to leave for China in February. "Oh, I think that's wonderful, honey! Just wonderful." She smiled and squeezed my arm. "Here. You will need a good umbrella. February is the rainy season down there. Take this one."

The Banquet

For months leading up to my departure, we got together for tea, practiced various Mandarin phrases, and browsed through her photo albums. Grandma had visited Guangxi province several years earlier, and had even made a tourist top in Yangshuo as a part of her boat tour of the Li River.

After having read so much about the breathtaking scenery in Yangshuo, I was almost star-struck when the first mountains crept up in the distance on my ride from the Guilin airport. They jutted out from the earth creating a jagged-tooth skyline like something from a fantasy story setting. As we drove into Yangshuo, the green-grey hills loomed above, ahead and behind us. I pressed my face to the grimy window. The cab driver yawned.

Yangshuo appeared on the tourist radar when foreign and Chinese backpackers alike flocked there for the scenery, fresh air, and friendly locals. Where there were foreigners (from all around the world) the Chinese tourists soon followed and before long, Yangshuo, once a sleepy farming community, became a bustling tourism hot spot, complete with "West Street," the town's shopping district.

Thankfully, after being in Yangshuo for a few days, meeting some locals, and doing some exploring on my own, I was able to find all kinds of quiet corners, untouched by the tourist crowd. Any time I wanted some peace and quiet, I needed only to walk out of town for ten minutes into the breathtaking countryside, where I could stroll alongside straw-capped farmers trudging through fields with their water buffalos.

For the first three months I carried my camera everywhere I went. After Yangshuo began to feel more like home, I realized that some images would always stand out in my mind when I thought of this place, and I didn't always need pictures to remind me. Images like the little pig-tailed girl riding by me on her pink bicycle. She was humming and holding a stick with a long string attached, and at the end of the string—floating and fluttering like the most graceful of kites—was a yellow plastic bag. Or, on another walk into the countryside, there were the wrinkled ladies on the side of the road selling flower crowns for 2 Yuan (20 cents) to people out walking or riding their bikes. Another time, during a rainy walk, I saw a group of three small children with their arms around each other sharing their pink umbrella.

Then there were the sounds and smells. Our teacher accommodations were right at the edge of where Yangshuo spread out into the countryside, so in the spring and summer I got to fall asleep to the sound of frogs singing in the marshy ditches. It also meant the smells wafting around were a mix of wet pavement, marshy terraces, sour garbage, oily fried food, stale cigarettes, and for two glorious weeks in June, the fragrant smell of jasmine blossoms.

It took fifteen minutes to walk, or five minutes by bicycle to get anywhere around town. After being in Yangshuo a week, I knew all the back alleys and short cuts to my regular destinations, such as the vendor who sold me takeaway noodles in a plastic bag, and my favourite fruit markets.

As is the case with most tourist towns, Yangshuo continues to boom and develop around its signature mountains. By mid-summer, a KFC had been built at the top of West Street, a sign of things to come, no doubt.

I worked at a small English college with three American English teachers and one Chinese English teacher, who quickly became my good friend and unofficial tour guide. We had the freedom to run our own English programs, as long as they fit the class's abilities. Our students were young adults from all over China. I found the majority of them to be extremely motivated and determined to improve their English skills. Some were hoping to find better jobs, while others were working towards studying abroad. In the last five years, especially with Beijing hosting the Olympics, knowing how to speak English has become an invaluable credential.

On weekends the students and teachers went on expeditions together to see some of the sites around the area, some natural, some not. Always our students tried hard to improve their English, and learn as much as they could about the western world. They also did everything they could to befriend me, and my teacher colleagues.

On my first full day in Yangshuo, I met a fellow named Gary who gave me my Chinese name, Ai Mei Li (because it sounds like Emily), which means "Love Beautiful." He quickly became not only one of my best friends in Yangshuo, but my Chinese language/culture teacher. He loved going for walks in the countryside and having long conversations with me about our cultural differences.

After only a few days in Yangshuo, I knew that even though I'd passed up potential opportunities to work in Chengtu, I had found the place in China where I was supposed to be. It felt absolutely right.

Emily enjoying the view of Yangshuo, after climbing one of the many mountains. Photo by Emily Foster

Chapter 4

Treacherous Trip Home

1947

I was in school for five years, training to be a nurse at the University of Saskatoon. Career choices for girls in those days were pretty slim and I didn't want to be a secretary, or a teacher. For a time I was interested in being a commercial artist like my mother. As a child I used to follow her on her trips into rural China and watch as she sketched the local people in their surroundings.

When I told Mother about my aspirations to become an artist, she shook her head and told me, "Your passion doesn't lie in art. You need to work with people." It hurt a little, but I wasn't upset because I knew she was right. I did enjoy sewing, embroidery and knitting (I knit my first sweater when I was just 10 years old), but I wasn't consumed by the need to create works of art, like Mother was.

I took her advice and went into nursing (while taking occasional art classes on the side). The World Mission paid for my tuition at nursing college, and Mom and Dad gave us what little money they could spare for room and board.

On one of the occasions when Walton Tonge and I were visiting each other during a school holiday, a young boy in Griffin looked up at the two of us and asked loudly, "When are you getting married?"

Walton's ears glowed red. "Uhhhh, I uh...."

I said, "I don't know! He hasn't asked me yet!"

"Of course I'm going to ask you, when the time is right," Walton sputtered.

The right time turned out to be during my final year of training. Sitting in one of the student lounges, Walton bumbled his way through a sentimental speech about love and life, and then asked me to marry him. I had a terrible cough at the time, and kept interrupting him with my dry hacking. I accepted his proposal, and then promptly lent him money to help pay for my ring.

We planned to get married the following June, just after my graduation. It was 1945. The Second World War had ended, and my parents were coming home on furlough after seven years away. Seven years! I decided we should get married before my parents came home, in order to get all the mayhem over with. I wanted to devote my time and energy to my parents when they arrived, without wedding details mucking things up. Family and friends couldn't understand why I wasn't going to let my parents be a part of the ceremony. In all honesty, the wedding was a small part of my life at the time. My marriage was important to me, of course, but we kept the wedding day simple. We didn't have very much money. When my parents came home, after being away for so long, and having lived through the constant threat of Japanese invasion, I wanted to be able to completely devote myself to their company, rather than let myself be pulled in different directions because of wedding details.

For our honeymoon, friends of ours let us use their cottage in northern Ontario for two relaxing weeks. Afterwards, Walton and I moved to Toronto because he still had one more year of study before he could be ordained. I worked part-time as a critical care nurse, and was on call at various hospitals around the city. My parents, meanwhile, spent their furlough in Griffin, as usual.

Six months after arriving in Canada, Dad received word from Chengtu that the head worker he had left in charge of the printing press in his absence had died from a stroke. As much as Dad wanted to spend more time with his family, he felt the need to return to the mission field as soon as possible, before things began to unravel at the printing press. Mother decided to stay and finish the rest of her furlough in Griffin with her family on the farm. She was still in the middle of a number of painting projects, and wanted to complete them before joining Dad in China.

When I discovered I was pregnant, in the summer of 1946, I sent mother a package with some wool, knitting needles and a pattern for a baby's sweater. On the card I wrote, "Get knittin' Grandma, and not for Britain!"

A short time later, a month before our departure for China, Mother came and lived with Walton and me in Toronto. As much as I missed having Dad around, especially after our long-awaited reunion, it was delightful to live with my mother. For the first time in seven years, I was able to see her on a daily basis. Our jobs kept us busy, but in the evening, settling in for a cup of tea before bed, I never tired of her. Some young women would go crazy having their mothers live with them, especially during the first year of marriage! It was not so for me. My mother was so relaxed and accepting that it was impossible not to get along with her. She was helpful when I needed help, and distant when necessary. It was our time in Toronto that brought mother and me together as friends.

Beatrice hard at work in Toronto. 1945. Photo by John Kitchen.

Before the wedding, I had made myself a comfortable nightie for my honeymoon. With lace at the collar and cuffs billowing sleeves, it turned out to be more like a large flannel tent than a garment. The fabric was pale green with small pink roses, and was soft and cozy.

As it turned out, I didn't wear it on our honeymoon because I was given a couple of slinky nighties for wedding presents from friends. My enormous green nightie was also far too warm for evenings in June.

When Mother came to live with us, the nights became quite cool so I lent her my nightie. Mother's frame was smaller than mine, so it looked ridiculous on her, like a moo-moo on a small child. She wore it every night. And when we packed everything up for China, the nightie was lovingly stowed away in her trunk.

When Walton was finally ordained in 1946, the United Church accepted him to the mission field in West China. We planned to leave for China with Mother in the summer, at the end of her furlough.

After months and months of delay (in post-war times, international travel was anything but reliable), we found ourselves in San Francisco not in summer as we had planned, but in December. By this time I was seven months pregnant.

Walton, Mother and I were a part of the largest group of missionaries ever to leave together for the Far East. We totaled about nine hundred people from different denominations and religions.

Our ship, the Marine Lynx (or *Marine Stinks*, as it soon became known), had been built for transporting American soldiers, so style and comfort hadn't been considered in its design. We had been instructed not to bring many belongings because there wasn't any room on the ship to store much of anything. The sleeping decks consisted of triple bunk beds pressed together on one side, with two feet of space on the other. We were crammed together like books on a shelf. We didn't have any chairs to sit on and we couldn't sit on the bunks because they were too low. The only break from standing around was lying down. Pregnant women in their last trimester need to sit down a lot, so I was uncomfortable most of the time on that ship. Thankfully we brought our own foldout chairs for sitting on the upper deck when we needed some air.

Mother and I decided to sleep down on the fifth deck with five hundred or so other mothers and children. Next to the sleeping quarters was the kitchen. We thought there would be refreshing drafts of air drifting through the passageway to the kitchen. I don't know where that notion came from. Probably Mother. In any case, it was a terrible idea. People were constantly coming and going from the kitchen at all hours of the day and night. We were forced to tolerate yells and smells, clanging and banging, and a steady stream of fathers coming down to visit their wives and children. Privacy, as it turned out, was one of many luxuries we had left on shore.

After a week or so at sea, the air around our bunks on the fifth deck was sour with a smelly mix of vomit, dirty diapers and oily noodles.

Women strung ropes around the bunks to make crib-like cages to keep their young children from falling out of bed. My bunk happened to be pressed up against a toddler's bed. I often woke with the baby curled up beside me on my bunk. More often then not she was wet and smelled of urine.

Three weeks on the *Marine Stinks* felt like three long months.

Thankfully I didn't have to contend with seasickness like almost everyone else on board. Even the captain's skin eventually took on a greenish-yellow tinge. As the ship rocked back and forth through several days of a typhoon, poor Walton couldn't get up from his bunk. Mother was indisposed for a while as well.

We had to line up like cattle outside the kitchen for meals. The food was slopped onto our trays in lumpy spoonfuls. We ate a lot of soupy mashed potatoes mixed in with canned peaches. Yet, despite the less-than-perfect conditions on the ship, I don't recall hearing complaints from anybody. Maybe they were all too sick. I don't know.

The bathroom on the fifth deck was a bare, open room with rows of dirt-speckled sinks down one wall. The back wall opened into the engine room, where sweaty men worked, averting their eyes from the women doing their business. Toilets were lined up side by side with no walls between them. Next to the toilets were the communal showers, minus the shower curtains. I quickly got used to living so openly, but I felt sorry for the Catholic nuns, many of whom would wait until the early hours of the morning to shower or use the toilets. Mother did as well, come to think of it.

Walton became terribly frustrated in the third deck men's quarters because of the many prayers that took place at different times of day. Just when one fellow's chanting and bowing would end, another man would get out of bed to begin his ritual. Every denomination was on a different schedule. Many men grumbled about the lack of sleep for the first week at sea. Finally they came up with a compromise. For the duration of the journey, the men would pray in silence, out of respect for a good night's slumber.

By the time Christmas rolled around, most people didn't know or care what day it was because they were so seasick. My mother and I, however, did what we could to make the most of what little we had. I collected bits of raw macaroni from the kitchen, and pieces of string from the floor, and filled one of Walton's socks. In the early morning I hung the "stocking" next to his bed. Walton's bunk neighbours enjoyed watching him pull the presents from his sock. He entertained them by crying out with glee, as if the macaroni was exactly what he had always wanted.

Meanwhile, I was on the deck below, opening my present from Mother. It was a five-cent drawing pencil that I continued to use until it was a stub too small for my fingers.

I almost cried when we finally reached the Shanghai port. I'd never been so happy to get off of a ship and onto solid ground! We could feel the stale air inside the decks suddenly become electric with excitement. However, it wasn't going to be as quick and simple to leave as we'd hoped. As we lined up at the exits to file off the ship, we were unwittingly stepping from one trying situation into another.

The Japanese had changed the laws of the land, and even though the war was over and the Japanese soldiers were gone, their rules still applied. One such rule dictated that no drugs or cosmetics be allowed into the country, not even handcreams as one young missionary on our ship discovered. Before we'd even had a chance to get off the ship, the poor woman was roughly whisked away for questioning. The customs agents then decided that it was necessary to search all passengers coming off the Marine Lynx. They came on board and searched us one by one.

Dr. Ted Wilford, a fellow traveler on his way to West China, had approximately $5000 worth of radium stored in four lead blocks. Radium was used in those days to treat cancer. Because of the radioactive nature of radium, it was highly illegal and had to be smuggled into China. The heavy lead blocks were stored in the pockets of two raincoats hanging neatly over Dr. Wilford's arm. When he heard the custom's agents coming on board, he quickly made a plan, and then asked for our help.

The fifteen of us who were headed for West China pressed together in a tight pack as the officers searched through our trunks and handbags. Before they could frisk Dr. Wilford, he passed his raincoat back to Walton, who was standing directly behind him. Before Walton was searched, he passed the raincoat to me, and then I passed it on to my neighbour. And so it went, and in this way the illegal radium went undetected.

However, we soon realized it was not so easy. After they finished searching our bags, an officer led us down a narrow gangplank towards another wall of surly customs agents, ready to frisk us as we passed.

After deciding against throwing the toxic radium into the harbour, Dr. Wilford held his head high, and led the way down the gangplank. The line of uniformed customs agents looked up at us expectantly. Suddenly one of the men brightened as he saw Dr. Wilford. He greeted the doctor in English and held out his hand. I watched Dr. Wilford's face relax into a warm smile. It turned out that the friendly customs agent was a former English student of his. Apparently, the good doctor had made quite a difference in this particular student's life. The friendly young man waved our entire party through the line, exempting us from the final frisking process. Later that night (after the radium had been safely stashed away) Dr. Wilford took all fifteen of our group out for dinner.

And so ended our journey on the Marine Stinks. We learned later that the United States government scuttled her not long after we arrived in Shanghai. Our three-week adventure was the last voyage for that old bucket of bolts.

Our next plan was to catch a flight from Shanghai to Chengtu. Unfortunately, because so many planes had been used in the Second World War and hadn't been properly maintained, domestic flights at the time were few and far between. So Mother, Walton, and I found ourselves spending the first part of January in a Shanghai YMCA, in a room without heat. While we were stranded in Shanghai, Mother befriended a young missionary family embarking on their first trip to China. They had a toddler and an infant. Mother sat with them, helped with the children, and eased their anxiety about living in the Far East.

Meanwhile, Walton and I were getting nervous. Shanghai was the most expensive city in China at the time. If I were to give birth in Shanghai, the medical bill would be astronomical and the pittance Walton was paid could only be stretched so far. Walton and I didn't sleep very well for weeks. Our bags were packed, ready to leave at the first hint of a flight. Our shoes were always waiting expectantly by the door. If a plane became available, there would be no time to lose.

Despite our dwindling funds, Walton found the need to splurge on a used German camera in Shanghai, his first major purchase in Asia. Instantly it became his most prized possession. We didn't know it at the time, but that camera was going to come in very handy for us back in Canada.

Luckily we had few belongings. We actually had less than when we left San Francisco, thanks to a fire in the storage area at the Shanghai harbour. Because the room had been flooded to put out the fire, everything was soaked, including all of our luggage and the cast iron stove we'd brought for cooking. The stove was full of water and covered in rust, so we left it behind.

Unfortunately, all of our teacups went missing (likely stolen by customs people rummaging through our trunks, looking for illegal substances like hand-cream) so we ended up leaving our box of saucers behind as well. What good would saucers be without matching teacups?

Many missionaries were taking boats up river to get out of the city, but I couldn't take such a risk. Going into labour on a dirty riverboat could have meant serious infections, and possibly death for myself, or the baby. After waiting around for a month in Shanghai however, I was starting to think that taking a boat up river might be the only way out of the city. A day or two later, the airport finally summoned us. A plane was ready to take us to West China at last!

The crowd of excited missionaries stood closely packed together, waiting to get their hands on plane tickets. I remember being sandwiched between Walton and Mother, and feeling the tension escape like steam when we finally purchased our tickets. Everything was going to be all right after all.

On our way back to the YMCA, a tall woman with a pinched expression approached us. It was Dr. Cresswell, whom I recognized from our trip aboard the Marine Lynx. She explained that her hospital in Szechuan needed her desperately. "I was called away from the country, and my replacement has fallen ill. They have been without a doctor for nearly a month!"

Dr. Cresswell's plane was leaving the day after ours, but she was in too much of a hurry to wait any longer. She pleaded for someone to give up his or her seat on the first plane out. Mother volunteered without hesitation, saying she would stay behind and help the new missionary families she'd befriended. It didn't make much difference to her if she arrived in Chengtu a day late, whereas I, the pregnant one, needed to get to out of Shanghai as quickly as possible.

Before Walton and I departed, Mother insisted that I take the valuable gold watch she was carrying for a general's wife in West China. Without much of a postal service, missionaries traveling back and forth often acted as delivery agents for wealthy folks in third world countries. Mother had been asked to bring this spectacular gold watch from Canada to Chengtu. She took my cheap watch, with its fake leather strap, as a replacement. I thought the timing of the exchange was odd. "What difference does it make if the watch arrives a day or two late?" I asked her.

She shrugged and said, "It could make a difference to the general's wife. You never know."

Mother had never insured anything in her life. However, just before Walton and I boarded the plane, she approached us with a big smile on her face because she had just insured her trunk, and mailed the insurance papers to herself in Chengtu.

"Why did you do that?" Walton asked her.

She smiled, pleased with herself. "Why not? Nothing wrong with trying something new!"

The next morning, Walton and I rose to leave at three in the morning. Before leaving the room, I looked over at my mother who was sound asleep, curled up in her blanket. She had asked me the night before to wake her up to say goodbye, but I couldn't bring myself to disturb her. Her breathing was soft and deep, and her cheek was resting gently on her hand. I kissed her lightly on her forehead, then turned and closed the door quietly behind me.

Our plan was to fly into Chungking, and then out to Chengtu, but we had to wait a few days in Chungking before our plane to Chengtu was available. Luckily we had a missionary connection in Chungking who was nice enough to let us stay with him for the duration of the delay.

Unfortunately, when we got to the airport in Chungking, Walton and I were weighed along with our luggage, and told that we were too heavy. They only had room on the plane for one of us without any of the luggage.

What could we do but sigh deeply and comply? Complaining at that point was futile, and would have taken energy that we just didn't have. Walton decided he would return to the mission secretary's house and wait for my mother who was due to arrive the next day. Perhaps it would work out that the two of them could then fly to Chengtu together.

I watched Walton from the smudged window of the plane, and felt a flutter in my stomach, knowing that he couldn't speak a word of Mandarin except, "I love you" (Wo ai ni), and "Don't want" (Bu yao). I could see his lips moving, saying; "Bu yao" as the pack of coolies circled my husband and our pile of luggage, ready to grab anything they could get their hands on. I had no idea how he was going to get back to the mission secretary's house by himself. I felt completely helpless. There we were: Mother in Shanghai, father anxiously waiting in Chengtu, Walton stuck in Chungking, and me on a plane, with nothing to do but wait.

After my plane took off, a friendly officer assisted Walton in hailing a rickshaw to get him back to the mission secretary's house. The next day, Walton went to the airport to wait for a plane that carried missionary passengers and was due to arrive from Shanghai. He had no way of knowing for certain when it would arrive, or whether or not mother would be aboard.

While Walton was waiting, he noticed that the airport workers spoke in morose whispers, heads hanging low. A short time later, he overheard an official speaking in English to a pilot over the radio. "Go back! Go back!"

After a few minutes, the English-speaking officer approached Walton and told him quietly that they'd lost a plane.

"Where? How?"

"We don't know the details yet. We've lost contact with them. We think it's gone down."

Walton paced back and forth, surveying the cloudless sky for a plane. Without having any way to communicate with Father and me in Chengtu, Walton had no choice but to stay wait.

Several other planes arrived that afternoon, but there was no sign of my mother. Walton recognized a young missionary family at one point, and felt a rush of relief, remembering that Mother was supposed to be with them on their plane. When he approached them, they informed him that one of their kids had been ill, so they had switched tickets with another family in order to fly out earlier to seek medical treatment. They thought Mother had gone with another family on a different plane.

Meanwhile, I was at the mission compound in Chengtu with my father, in great spirits. It had been ten years since I was last in my hometown. I felt delighted to see the familiar streets lively with rickshaws, bicycles and pedestrians once again. Much of the city looked the same, with the exception of several buildings the Japanese bombs had reduced to rubble. The church we attended as children no longer had a roof, and the lovely wooden floor, exposed to the elements, had rotted away. However, they were slowly rebuilding, and the people of Chengtu seemed to carry on as usual.

Open stores with their colourful wares spilled onto the sidewalks. I inhaled deeply the familiar smokey smell of charcoal stoves and simmering spices. Skeletal dogs ran everywhere, nosing through piles of garbage. Temple bells rang in the distance.

The morning after my arrival, Dad hadn't touched his breakfast. I noticed that he kept disappearing to talk to the mission secretary. I found out later that while they'd heard about a plane crash, they didn't have any details about who was on the plane, and were therefore keeping things quiet. We were all in the dark.

On Thursday morning, almost three days after I'd arrived in Chengtu, Dad gently knocked on my bedroom door. I rolled over, my belly protruding upward like a rolling hill under the blanket. "Good morning Dad." I rubbed my eyes and propped myself up a little as Dad took a seat on the edge of my bed. I saw his red-rimmed eyes and felt the kick of dread in my chest.

"Muriel, we have terrible news," came a woman's soft voice from the doorway, one of the other missionary wives from the area. She walked into my room and placed a hand on Dad's shoulder. Her eyes were also red. I remember feeling something rush and then drain inside me, followed by the need to sink into the mattress. I shook my head, looking at Dad's downcast face. A tear dripped from his eye onto my blanket.

In a whisper, he told me that a plane from Shanghai, flying to Chungking had crashed in a field near a small town. One soul had survived, but none of the people on the plane had been identified, and no one was sure who the survivor was.

I took a deep breath and said to Dad, "If she survived the plane crash, she will probably be paralyzed, or mutilated and in severe pain." My voice cracked and I felt myself giving into the mattress. "So, I hope it's not her."

Many of the planes were in poor condition and hadn't been serviced since before the war. The engine in Mother's plane caught fire. The pilots tried to land, but crashed into a field next to the small town of *Tien Men*, (which means *Gateway to Heaven*). Villagers below could see passengers leaping from the plane, falling to their deaths. One of those who jumped was my mother. The passengers who stayed on the plane were burned beyond recognition.

Bandits had stripped most of those who jumped before the authorities arrived. Investigators found my mother in the brush beside the field, lying on her back. Her money belt and the leather watch had been stolen. Underneath her sweater, still nestled beneath her arm, was a screaming infant. He had a concussion, two broken legs, and was paralyzed on one side of his face, but he was alive! He was the youngest member of one of the families Mother had helped in Shanghai. She must have grabbed him when the plane went down and clutched him to her chest before she jumped. He was the only one to survive the crash.

Once found, he was taken to a nearby hospital, where missionaries came to fetch him a short time later. He was later taken back to the United States to be reunited with his grandparents. I tried for a while to track him down, but didn't have any success. We were told that his Grandparents had passed on the heroic story to him, but altered it slightly, so that it was the baby's mother who jumped from the plane to save his life. We didn't mind the alternate ending. I decided to leave well enough alone, and gave up my search.

A short time after the crash, Walton and I were reunited in Chengtu, where we stayed with Dad, all of us crushed with grief. The despair was unlike anything I had ever experienced. Being in China without my mother felt horribly wrong. I saw her face everywhere around the compound, and the least little thing, like a bird landing on an outstretched branch, reminded me of her.

We were unable to attend the funeral service, or retrieve my mother's remains because all planes were grounded once again due to the crash. Mother and the other missionaries who died in the crash were buried in the International Cemetery in Wuhan.

Because of the ticket trading that had gone on prior to flights taking off from Shanghai, none of the officials really knew who was on the flight. It took several days of investigating to finally get the facts sorted out. At first, it was presumed that Walton and I were also on the flight with Mother. Luckily, our immediate relatives in Canada had heard from us before they got wind of the radio news flash announcing that we had all perished. For a short time, there were still friends and extended family who believed we were dead. The mess took a few weeks, and a lot of telegrams back and forth, to clear up.

One of the many articles written about Beatrice Kitchen and the plane crash. 1947. Published in the United Church Observer.

A family friend had been able to visit the cemetery, so he sent us photographs of mother's grave. Mother's gravestone was right next to a flourishing sycamore tree in front of a small chapel. Walton, Dad and

I had plans to see it one day, once the airplanes were up and running again. Later on, however, when the Communists took over the country, all the cemeteries in China were removed or flattened. We were told that soldiers took the headstones, broke them in two and built sitting stools out of them. Still, we hoped to someday visit the site where my mother was buried.

The first time we returned to China in 1981, we couldn't find the old International Cemetery. During our second visit in 1988, however, we found a large housing storage site, built over what had once been the cemetery. We were fairly certain that the Communists wouldn't have built residential houses over the gravesite because of the deeply rooted Chinese fear of spirits. The small chapel had been repainted, and was being used as the office for a housing development, but mother's sycamore tree was there, taller and even more beautiful, with branches that reached out and welcomed us. Beside the tree was a small shed made of bricks and cement. I asked one of the men working at the storage space what it was. "For paint," he said. "Bandits kept breaking into the main building and stealing our buckets of paint, so we had to build this little shed to keep them out."

My mother would have loved the sycamore tree.

A month after mother's death, I gave birth to a beautiful baby girl. As she curled her tiny pink hand around my finger, my shattered heart swelled with love. I wanted to emulate all that my mother had been, as best I could. I wanted to name our daughter Beatrice, but she'd made me promise years before that I wouldn't burden any of my children with her name. She'd hated it. So we settled on using mother's middle name, Irene, and chose a name that both Walton and I liked, Leslie. So, that's how your mom became *Leslie Irene Tonge*.

My mother's belongings arrived in Chengtu a few days after her plane crashed, having been sent in a large trunk of supplies on a different plane.

In due time, Dad started looking around for women who might be interested in taking mother's clothes. He called on Mrs. Miller who was the wife of an Austrian doctor who had been adopted by our mission. He had fled Europe during the war, and didn't have anywhere to turn to when the dust settled. Their homeland was in ruins, and they didn't have passports, so the Millers had no choice but to stay in China for a while.

Dr. and Mrs. Miller visited my father to express their deepest sympathies after the crash, and Dad promptly directed them to our attic, telling them to help themselves to any of my mother's things. I arrived shortly afterward to find Dad seated at the kitchen table, his hands folded neatly in his lap, his eyes downcast and shadowed.

"What can I do to help you, Dad?" I asked.

"Why don't you go upstairs and see if you can help the Millers with mother's belongings."

As I climbed the stairs to the attic, I heard laughter and a shuffling sound on the floor. I poked my head up into the attic and saw Mrs. Miller singing and dancing amid the dusty boxes and open trunks. She wore my green honeymoon nightie over her clothes, like a little girl exploring a trunk of dress-up clothes. Mr. Miller sat on a nearby trunk, laughing. They stopped when they heard the creaky floorboards under my feet.

"Muriel, whoever would make such an enormous nightie?" asked Mr. Miller, grinning at me.

"You know," said Mrs. Miller, "I haven't been able to buy any new clothes for either of my daughters since we arrived. But I'd say there is enough material in this nightie for two little dresses, wouldn't you, Muriel?"

I thought of my tiny mother, snuggled up in a chair, wearing my honeymoon nightie. "I think you're right," I said to Mrs. Miller.

I could barely eat supper that night. Why hadn't I stood up for myself and told them that the nightie was mine, that I had made it and that my mother had loved it? It had been her favourite thing to wear to bed, even though it was ugly and enormous. How could I have let the Millers take it away, without letting them know how much it meant to me?

Dad looked across the table at me and put down his fork. "Is something the matter, Muriel?"

I was openly crying by the time I'd finished explaining how I felt. Walton banged his hand on the table and said, "Go get it back! It wasn't even hers to be given away. It is yours! *You* made it. You haven't even had a chance to wear it yet!"

I lowered my head. It was too late. The Millers had been so excited about making new dresses for their girls. For all I knew, Mrs. Miller had already cut up the fabric.

As it turned out, I was right.

The next Sunday, I went to church as usual, only this Sunday was different. This time there were two little girls sitting in the front pew, grinning from ear to ear, looking radiant in their matching pale green dresses, with white lace around the collars and cuffs. Mrs. Miller sat proudly beside them, hands folded in her lap.

She looked over and smiled at me, and I felt the warmth of my mother spread though my whole body. I smiled back.

Chapter 5

A Western Housewife

"How are you doing honey? Do you need a snack?"
"No, I'm good Grandma, thanks. How are you?" I looked down at Grandma's hands. She was lightly fingering one of the yellowed newspaper articles about the plane crash.
"Fine, fine. Should I just keep going then? Where was I?"
"You just had my mom." A twittering bird flew across the square of sky above her yard. Grandma and I both watched it land on a tree branch above our heads.
"Oh yes. March 18th, 1947. You know, when your mom was born, there were two clocks that said different times in the hospital room? One said 11:59 p.m., and the other said 12:01. So the doctor let me choose which date I wanted for you mom's birthday. Since March 17th was already a special day for St. Patrick, I decided that my daughter would need her own special day for when she is famous someday. So her birthday is on the 18th. Did you know that?"
"Yes."
I have heard that story at least once a year ... usually around mom's birthday. I smiled at Grandma and put my hand over hers.

My grandma is adorably stout. Everything about her physique is short, including her fingers and toes. She has a broad smile and warm brown eyes so large you can see right into her enormous heart.

Since Granddad Walton died of heart failure in 1994, she has lived alone in their Toronto home. Now, at age 86, she fills her days with taking care of everyone around her, including people in nursing homes who are younger than she is. She is an active member of her church congregation, and her community. She still speaks to groups around Toronto about her experiences in China, and captivates complete strangers with her stories.

Her four children and their spouses all lovingly tease Grandma every chance they get. In fact, she takes more kidding than anyone I know. In the face of gentle ridicule, she holds her head high, and always says something like: "I don't pay attention to comments from the cheap seats." She loves to remind me that it's important to laugh at oneself, and, "You can always get further in life with a sense of humour."

The walls of Grandma's house are covered with her oil paintings, hanging slightly askew, landscapes featuring disproportionately large ducks as well as several China-inspired paintings as well, like the one of a skinny Chinese fisher-boy, wearing a Chinese hat, and tattered pants.

One of her bookshelves is stocked with books about China given to her by friends over the years. She never reads them because why read about it when you've seen it first hand? For entertainment, she'd rather read touching stories about heroic animals in *Reader's Digest* Magazine, or watch a James Bond movie, or better yet, a baseball game. Grandma is one of the Toronto Blue Jays' most faithful fans.

On the day of our first formal interview, I peeked into the television room and saw the heaps of photo albums on the floor. Grandma had been digging around looking for pictures and clippings to show me. She called me into the kitchen, where she was cooking a casserole of some sort. I could smell the top layer of cheese browning and bubbling. She took my hand and led me down to the basement for a quick showing of her latest sewing project: some dolls for the church bazaar. She had boxes of old knitting magazines and patterns from the seventies stacked in all corners, along with piles of folded sheets of colourful fabric. Freckles of wool and sewing bits covered the carpet, remnants of past projects, and works in progress. If you ever needed something from the basement, Grandma had to navigate around and find it for you, and it usually took a while.

"Are you sure you wouldn't rather do this inside, Emily? Are you warm enough out here?"

"I'm fine," I said, turning my face up to the flawless April sky. "The sun is nice and warm."

Grandma put a plate of fresh buttered rolls on top of my notebook and sat in the patio chair beside me. "Are you sure honey? We could go back into the kitchen if you're cold."

I shook my head. "This is fine. Good thinking, doing this outside." I moved the plate of rolls and opened my notebook to a fresh page.

Grandma propped her elbow onto the patio table and glanced down at the small square of garden beside us. Tiny heads of green were beginning to poke out of the wet earth. I bit into the warm roll.

*

1948

Our first year back in China, Walton and I lived with Dad in Chengtu at the mission compound, where we studied Mandarin for a year. Our only professional obligation at that time was language study, which left us ample time to look after our precious new daughter. I didn't have trouble figuring out the Mandarin vocabulary, having grown up in Chengtu, but my challenge was learning the proper pronunciations, and formal grammar, because I had grown up listening to the local language.

Let me tell you, caring for a tiny baby in rural China back then was no easy task. Leslie didn't have any toys, mobiles, cribs, carriages, disposable diapers or jars of baby food. Walton's wages were so slight that I had to make or scrounge for everything the baby needed. Someone gave me the big wheels of an old English Pram, and I had a top for it built at a wicker factory. Leslie slept in a homemade crib with screening along the sides and top to keep the mosquitoes and rats out.

Lin Da Neong, dear soul, had been our amah throughout my childhood in China. She had chased around after us, made sure we ate properly, and had humoured us in our games and antics. After mother's death, Lin Da Neong once again became an extremely important part of our family, helping to look after Dad, Leslie and me. I hadn't realized how very hard she worked.

I remember her feeling strongly that I should have a daily glass of hot milk, mid-morning. Every day she would boil up some fresh milk, then walk all over the compound until she found me. Trouble was that by the time she had tracked me down, the milk had usually cooled and there would be a thick scummy layer on the top, peppered with dust and tiny bugs. Lin Da Neong refused to leave me alone until I had downed the milk so I was forced to pinch the scum out of the glass, toss it on the grass, hold my breath and gulp the foul liquid down. By that point, it usually smelled like a cow had stepped into the glass, but the milk was good for me and Lin knew it.

A year after our arrival in Chengtu, Walton and I were sent to Juenhsien, to one of the mission stations there. It was the same rural town where I had been born twenty-six years earlier. Here, we were to continue our language study and be eased into our work as missionaries. It was 1948.

As I child, I had grown up with amahs and cooks who cared for us, prepared our meals and tended to housekeeping chores. One of their jobs was to go to the market to buy whatever fresh produce was in season. Since we didn't have refrigerators, there were daily trips to the marketplace. If I had gone to the market to stock up on eggs, you can bet the price would have tripled when the merchants took one look at me. Also, when I would try to walk through the market, the crowd that gathered and followed me around was intrusive and irritating. Imagine going to the grocery store and hardly being able to move in the aisles because of the packs of people watching your every move!

That's but one tiny example of why we appreciated household help, but believe me, there were many more. It would have been seen as an insult to the community if we had not provided jobs for cooks and amahs. Chinese people thought western missionaries could afford to hire help, and that they treated their household help with kindness and respect, so amah and cooking jobs were much in demand. Also, the simple truth of the matter is that we missionaries couldn't have done our jobs without some help in the home.

I only had one baby, this is true, but housekeeping was a full time job in rural China. I remember as a child in Chengtu watching our cook refine brown sugar. He had a large cauldron filled with sugar boiling in water. The dirty froth was skimmed off the top and egg shells were thrown in to aid in collecting the dirt. I also remember our cook sifting the flour to get rid of all the tiny black bugs.

We kept yeast alive in jars, to be used later in baking bread. Butter was hand-made. Water was always boiled. Milk had to be boiled too, and was then lowered down into our well to be kept cool.

A sample menu of what our cook would make for us (with a little help from me) looked like this:

Breakfast:
-Cooked cereals (oats were ground in stone grinder so there were always little bits of grit and stones in the oatmeal!)

-Fresh baked bread
-Ground rice cereal
-Eggs and toast
-Pancakes (syrup made with sugar, water, vanilla and maple flavouring)

Lunch:
-Soups (watered down)
-Sandwiches (with home-made peanut butter!)
-Egg dishes

Dinner:
-Lots of rice
-Overcooked meat (chicken, mostly) from the market
-Fresh vegetables in season from the garden such as tomatoes, string beans, and
   cucumbers.

We stuck to what we knew, I suppose. I now think it is interesting how little Chinese food our cooks made for us. I did eat a lot of Chinese pickles.

In Juenhsien, Walton and I hired a cook who took very good care of us. Servants and cooks had many opportunities to cheat their employers, so you were blessed if you had a trusting relationship with your hired help. Friends of mine worried all the time that their servants were pocketing some of the errand money, or that some servants were buying lower cuts of meat and then recording higher prices in the accounting books. Getting watered down milk was fairly commonplace. Walton and I eventually had our own cow for fresh supplies of milk, which was handy when we needed to make butter. Many others around town weren't so fortunate.

One missionary I knew got fed up with receiving watery milk, so one day he insisted that the local milkman bring his cow and milk to the front of his house where he could observe the milking carefully to be sure he wasn't being cheated. Before committing to buying the milk, he insisted on having a small taste. The milkman obliged. The missionary drank a small cup full and spat it out on the ground. It was still watery! How could watery milk be coming out of the cow's teat? After careful inspection, he discovered that the milkman had perfected an ingenious scheme for those occasions when he was called to a customer's house. He stashed a hot water bottle under his arm, and hid a small plastic tube attached to the hot water bottle up his sleeve. With each squeeze of the cow's teat, the milkman applied a little pressure to the hot water bottle, sending a squirt of warm water down the tube, into his hand, and into the stream of milk. The missionary was flabbergasted!

I remember another missionary couple complaining that their milk was always being watered down. They confronted the milkman, who insisted that the milk directly came from the cow. Then one day the couple found tadpoles swimming around in their milk jug! I'm pretty sure they bought their own cow after that.

The folks who delivered our coal for heating had several ways to swindle us. I heard stories about some of them painting rocks black to weigh down the coal basket, or soaking the coal and basket in water so it appeared to weigh more. Some people were accused of pocketing lumps of coal after a basket had been purchased and adding the stolen lumps to the next basket. It was hard to keep up!

Many of my missionary friends tried their best to stay on top of such things, but I decided early on that I had no interest in counting the eggs, or weighing the meat, or locking the pantry. I was both overly trusting and just plain lazy. I did not run a very strict household. As I have often said, I didn't know what the heck I was doing much of the time. I thought that if someone needed coal or flour or milk that badly, then they should take it. I didn't care all that much.

When we moved up to a mountain cottage to escape the summer heat, it didn't take long for word to spread among the locals that a health-care professional was in their midst. I had a Red Cross box of medical supplies that I took with me everywhere we went. That summer in the mountains, I was pregnant again but still stayed busy around the community where I could, rather than stay home and keep house.

When I refer to our mountain cottage, by the way, I don't want to give the wrong impression. The cottages were mountain shacks, where multiple rooms and furniture were a luxury. There was no electricity, running water or even screened windows.

Whenever I heard about people in the mountain village suffering from various ailments, I would pack up my little Red Cross box and head out to help where I could with bandages, disinfectant, stitches, and whatever other supplies were available. Local folks started lining up outside our door. Over the span of a few days, our cottage became a small clinic of sorts, and everyone seemed to know who we were.

The most serious case I dealt with that summer was an elderly man whose back was blanketed with lumpy carbuncles. His family carried him up to our cottage in a *whagan*, which is a type of stretcher. He was very sick, and had developed a fever. I remember my hands trembling as I looked over the raw flesh on his back and began to treat the infection as best I could. His family carried him up every day for two weeks to see me. I used up all the bandages and gauze in my Red Cross kit, trying to help him. I had to resort to ripping up our spare bed sheets, and when those ran out I started using old newspapers that were leftover from the last renters of the cottage. Eventually the elderly gentleman was able to shuffle up to our cottage on his own to see me. I went down the mountain to his family's farm one day to pay him a surprise visit. Well, you can imagine the greeting I received. His family members were ever so gracious and kind. I remember the tears in their eyes as they squeezed my hands, thanking me profusely.

One night, after returning home from visiting with a sick neighbour, Walton and I heard shouts and gunshots coming from down the mountain. We knew the dangers of bandits in the area, but had never seen them first hand. Walton and I ran to each other, eyes wide with dread. Instinctively, I covered my belly with my arms, and pulled Leslie close to me. Friends had told us stories about bandits breaking into homes and beating all the family members.

Walton and I listened to the commotion for a moment. Women screaming, men shouting, gunshots echoing over the mountain ... it had to be bandits. From our windows we could see people running into the hills, abandoning their houses and belongings.

Walton and I closed the shutters.

"What do we do?" I asked, cringing as I heard another gunshot. I picked Leslie up and held her tightly to my chest.

Walton wordlessly grabbed our two most prized possessions: a small dented typewriter, and the used German camera he'd bought in Shanghai when we'd first arrived. He stashed them at the back of one of the kitchen cupboards. "Take Leslie and run down the mountains. Hide in the bushes until things have quieted down up here," he instructed.

"I'm not going down the mountain at night! There are tigers, Walton!"

Leslie began to whimper.

"Just do it, Muriel!" He grabbed me by the elbow and pulled me toward the door.

"What are you going to do? What happens if the bandits come in here?"

"I'm going to find a club or something, and ward them off. Don't worry about me. Keep Leslie safe."

"Just wait one minute," I shouted over the noise, backing away from the door. "I'm *not* running into tiger territory, and you are *not* going to ward off bandits with a club. That's absolutely preposterous!"

"Then what do you propose we do?"

His mouth hung open as I took all of our money out of a little wooden chest. We had approximately the equivalent to 10 dollars Canadian to our name. I placed our savings on the dining table, in plain view. Then I took out some teacups, and began preparing the kettle.

"We'll be ready for them when they come," I told my husband, who gaped at me as if I were sprouting leaves out of my head. After a minute or two, he joined me at the table, our money in a skimpy pile between our teacups.

"You can preach to them while I tend to their wounds," I said calmly.

In silence we waited and prayed. Our hearts pounded. Slowly the noise from the farms below began to fade. One of the villagers came and peeked through a crack in the shutter, only to see us seated at the table sipping our tea. He told us the bandits had taken off down the hill. The coast was clear.

The story about Walton and I waiting expectantly inside our home instead of running into the woods soon became legend around our little mountain community. Missionaries and locals alike loved telling the story, and once even performed a little play called "The Bandits and the Tonges" at one of our community gatherings.

By the time summer ended, and all the missionaries had returned to their mission stations, I was six months pregnant with our second child. We made our way to Juenhsien only to find out that the country was quickly falling to the Communists. We had been unable to keep abreast of what had been going on because we didn't have television, radios or newspapers. Our only contact with the world outside the mission in Juenhsien was my father, who sent us letters every week from Chengtu. He hadn't mentioned that China was in political turmoil because he didn't want to needlessly worry us. Few people in those days knew the severity of the country's unrest, including my Dad. This, they seemed to feel, was just another political dispute that would eventually pass.

Another month went by, and I began making plans for my second birth. I didn't want to go into labour at the mission hospital in Juenhsien because I had seen how they sterilized their dirty linens with a cauldron crammed so full that the sheets on top didn't even get wet in the boiling water! Also, the Chinese doctor there didn't want anything to do with me because I was western. If something went wrong with the delivery, he was convinced that all of Canada would hunt him down.

Walton and I decided it would be best to make the journey down to Chengtu for my labour, where we knew I would be well taken care of during and after the delivery. The trip should have taken a couple of days, but because of politically-related complications, it dragged on longer than expected, and became a larger ordeal than any pregnant woman should ever have to endure.

*

Chapter 6

Exiled

2008

One of the reasons I went to China, besides the need to see where Grandma Tonge had grown up, was to see in the flesh, the people who had endured so much in the last half century. I found China's tumultuous history intriguing, and was excited to learn more about it. However, since the majority of my students were in their early twenties, much of China's modern historical events were little more than textbook knowledge to them. I asked a few of them once about whether or not they ever talked to their parents and grandparents about the rise of communism, or the events of the Cultural Revolution, and was surprised to find out that those topics rarely came up in their households. Many of China's youth have moved on, apparently, and some would say rightfully so. However, there is an enormous gap between my students and their parents' generation. Chinese culture is changing so rapidly; it's hard for many people who lived through the early days of New China to comprehend the mindset of China's modern youth. My urban students belonged to a generation that enjoys the privileged innocence that comes with living a relatively sheltered, happy life.

One example of the many differences between the generations was the attitude toward learning English. Many of my students lied to their parents about being away on business, or being posted for a temporary stay in another city. Several students had quit their jobs to complete two months of language study, and knew that their parents wouldn't understand the need for skills in English, and would think they had shamed the family. The older generation (especially those people living in more rural areas) prioritized having one steady job over learning a foreign language.

In Yangshuo, the plugs for learning English were everywhere. Messages such as *"The Key to Success is English"* were plastered on signs on the road out to the countryside. Whenever I went into town people would approach me with smiles, eager to practice their English.

Several of my students in their late twenties could recall life being different when they were children. Harreo—whose name he created by combining "Harry Potter" and "Romeo"—grew up in a small village where one old man had a television. "We kids used to always go to the old man's house after school to watch the fuzzy screen. It was different then. There was less money, and the cities were still small. There was more nature," he told me. Several of my female students admitted to wanting to be soldiers when they were young girls. Now they were hoping to move their way up in the business world.

When Grandma was a young girl in Chengtu in the 1930's, China was always on the brink of war: war with itself (warlords fighting warlords over territory) then war with the Japanese, followed by more wars with itself (Nationalists, headed up by Chiang Kai-shek, against Communists, under Mao Tse-tung).

For Grandma, and other missionary children who lived a sheltered life behind protective compound walls, war was a danger they didn't truly absorb. Even when she returned as a young mother, Grandma felt a sense of immunity to what was going on around her, similar to the way we feel about wars taking place on the other side of the world. There was little room for politics in her world. She was too busy worrying about raising her family, and helping those around her. Immediate problems took precedence over country affairs. It wasn't until the political turmoil began to affect her directly, becoming her immediate problem that Grandma truly understood the predicament they were in.

*

1949

We left Juenhsien for Chengtu about two weeks before our second baby was due. Under normal circumstances, the journey would have taken about a day. However, the first thirty miles out of the mountains I had to take a sedan chair. Any other mode of transportation would have been too bumpy, and could have induced labour. We certainly didn't want the baby coming any earlier than expected. Walton rode ahead of me in a rickshaw with your mom in his lap. The sedan chair was the smoothest but slowest choice for me.

For whatever reason, the only sedan chair we could find to rent was a bridal chair, decorated with cheerful red and gold ornaments. Poor Walton was so embarrassed! Whenever we stopped for a break, nearby villagers would come out to the road to try and get a peek at the bride. Imagine their surprise when they saw me stepping out of the chair, a very pregnant white woman! At the time, I was far too uncomfortable to appreciate the humour in the situation.

Finally we reached the town of Tzeliutsing (*zil-yoo-jin*), where there was road access, and where we expected to rent a car to take us the rest of the way to Chengtu. However, upon arriving we discovered that the Nationalist army had commandeered all the cars in town. Apparently they were in trouble, and needed all the help they could get in their fight against the Communists. At that point, we still had no idea how serious the political situation was in China. I don't think anybody did.

Luckily there was a missionary friend living nearby who invited us to stay with him. It took us four days to finally find a car (if you could even call it a car). It had no lights or brakes, patches on the tires were bolted on, and it ran on alcohol. The man driving assured us that we could get to Chengtu in one day. Good enough. Having to travel any longer in that rickety tin can might have made me nervous.

Walton, baby Leslie and I, stuffed ourselves into the back seat, with the driver and two other passengers in the front, a business manager and an engineer. We had no idea who these men were, or what their business was in Chengtu, and I can honestly say that we didn't care. We were not in the mood for idol small talk. Neither were they, I'm sure. All of us were anxious to get on our way.

We couldn't drive very quickly out of Tzeliutsing because the Nationalist army was on the move at that point. Hundreds of men dressed in dusty uniforms clogged up the road, hanging their heads and shuffling their feet.

I'd brought along a sterile delivery kit, just in case the baby came en route to Chengtu, but I wasn't at all excited about the prospect of having to use it. As each hour passed, I became more and more cranky as my patience ran out. Walton could sense my extreme discomfort and finally took it out on the grumbling mass of soldiers outside the car. "Let us pass!" he hollered out the window in Mandarin.

The men ignored us. So Walton yelled, "There's a pregnant woman in here about to go into labour! If she has the baby here on the road then it will be your fault, and you will have to help us take care of it! SO LET US THROUGH!"

Thankfully the men took pity and the crowd slowly parted.

We had fallen far behind schedule. We still had to cross a whole range of mountains before we could get to the plains of Chengtu, and it was going to take hours.

By the time we reached the mountains, night had fallen. Imagine driving along narrow mountain roads in a car without working brakes or lights, twisting and turning with no guardrail between our car and the cliffs! Sometimes the car had trouble getting up hills, so the two passengers in the front would have to get out and stop the backwards rolling by jamming wedges behind the tires. All in the dark!

When we finally approached a town, we thanked God that we were still alive, and our driver made the sensible decision to stop for the night. I was irritated that Walton and I didn't have our bedding (the driver of our car had told us we wouldn't need it), but I was grateful to be off that mountain road at last.

Walton soon recalled that Dr. Cresswell, the woman who had made the fateful ticket trade with my mother, lived close by. I'm sure, had she been there, she would have bent over backwards to make us comfortable, but unfortunately she was away at a conference. To my great relief the doorman had no problem letting us in. It was common practice in China for missionaries to leave their houses set up for guests, just in case someone needed a place to sleep. Walton and I did the same thing whenever we travelled for any length of time. Upon stepping into Dr. Cresswell's home, however, we discovered that all the wood in the house had just been varnished with a toxic Chinese substance called *Chi*. When I was very small, I once rested my arms on a table that had been varnished with Chi, and the skin on my arms went crusty and itchy and oozed a foul-smelling liquid. Heavily, we left Dr. Cresswell's home.

Our next option was the town inn where the room we were given had two small beds covered in straw and grass mat, and each came with one rock-hard pillow. Underneath each bed we found a *puhguy* (pooh-guy), which is a quilt made of heavy cotton. I pulled one out from under the bed, only to find it hopping with fleas and bed bugs. I stuffed the puhguy back safely under the bed and curled up with Leslie in my arms, lying back on the bare straw. I looked over at the window and saw a wall of puzzled Chinese faces peering in at us. The windows didn't have any curtains, so I had to do my best to pretend they weren't there.

Walton was already snoring in the bed across from Leslie and me. Rats scuttled around on the straw-mat ceiling above us. I couldn't sleep. The scratching and squeaking was too much for me to ignore. Every now and then a tuft of straw from the ceiling would drift down on me. Luckily, like her father, Leslie was a deep sleeper while I, on the other hand, tossed and turned all night.

The next day we stumbled out of the inn to find our driver with the other two passengers lighting a fire underneath our car. They had to heat the alcohol in order to start the car, they explained. It was something like a steam engine. A fire under a car wasn't something you saw every day. Heaving a deep breath and muttering a prayer, I shimmied into the backseat, hands resting on my belly.

Daylight made the drive much more tolerable. We were in Chengtu in no time, only to find the city in an uproar. Foreigners were clearing out of the country as quickly as they could. Men in wrinkled business suits were everywhere, lugging their belongings and hailing rickshaws. Women were carrying their screaming children, running in all directions.

Missionary societies held emergency meetings to decide on courses of action. Most missionaries were ordered to go home by their various organizations. The Communists had just taken Beijing, and Chengtu, being one of China's larger cities, was likely to be a target.

Walton and I faced a difficult decision. Friends advised us to leave right away and seek refuge in Hong Kong, like everyone else was doing. However, because of the recent rush of refugees from China into Hong Kong, we knew there wouldn't be anywhere for us to stay, and we didn't know anyone there who could help us out. I would likely have to give birth to our second child in one of the dirty emergency tents that had been set up to shelter the flood of Chinese refugees. On top of that, the journey to Hong Kong could be potentially hazardous for the baby. Once again I didn't want to risk going into labour en route.

We knew if Communist soldiers took Chengdu, they would force all westerners to evacuate. However, airplane cabins weren't pressurized properly, and we knew pilots didn't allow fragile newborns to travel by air. Our other choice was to evacuate by boat, but all the boats heading down the Yangtze were crammed with people trying to get out of China in a hurry. It would be quick way for the baby, Walton and me to catch an illness or infection.

My body was stiff and aching from constantly moving around. In retrospect, we probably should have listened to our friends and left for Hong Kong but at the time, and on top of all of our other reasons for staying put, my aching legs didn't want to take another step. Despite the risk of a Communist takeover, and possibly being evacuated, we decided to have the baby in Chengtu.

After moving into the missionary compound with my father, Walton decided that he would leave the next day to go back to Juenhsien to evacuate our belongings. First, however, he needed a good night's sleep. After kissing me goodnight, Walton whispered, "Whatever you do Muriel, don't go into labour tonight."

At around two in the morning my water broke, and I went into labour ten days early. Our compound was in the city of Chengtu, but the hospital was three miles outside the city, so we had a bit of a journey ahead of us.

My father protested our leaving. "You can't travel at this time of night," he said. "Soldiers are patrolling around everywhere, and it's pouring rain!"

"And who is going to deliver the baby, Dad? You?" I gritted my teeth through the searing pain of a contraction.

Groggily, the gateman hailed us two rickshaws, and after ten agonizing minutes Walton and I were on our way.

We arrived at the hospital and twenty minutes later, our son Murray was born. The nurses promptly took him from me and placed him in a small, rat-proof cage. Then, for the first time in two weeks since we'd left our little house in Juenhsien, I slept soundly. Finally.

After several emergency meetings all over China, the Board of World Mission decided that every small missionary station would be evacuated. Those people, who chose to stay, moved to the two large stations in Chungking and Chengtu. We chose to stay rather than flee like so many other missionary families because we didn't want to abandon our work, or our friends. We honestly felt that we would be fine. Chengtu already had enough missionaries (my father included), so Walton and I were sent to the mission compound in Chungking, where we would live through 1948 and 1949.

Walton was the supervising pastor of the Chungking mission church. He also taught English at the girls' and boys' schools. I stayed home and looked after our babies, doing what I could to offer my services as a nurse to the neighbouring mothers and their own newborns. It kept me busy.

I could never judge those Chinese mothers, but it was hard not to be shocked sometimes by what they did to their children because of various superstitions. For example, many women lost their newborns to what they called the "seven-day twitch," when their babies would convulse violently, then die, seven days after birth. It was likely tetanus that killed them, caused by infections of the umbilical cord. Back then, the practice of cutting the cord with rusty scissors or a dirty knife was prevalent in rural China.

More often than not, the young mothers didn't want me around for the birth of their babies because I was a white woman, and would probably bring bad luck to the child. I insisted, in those situations, that I be allowed to visit as soon after the birth as possible at least, so that I could cut, clean, and retie the umbilical cord.

On one occasion I was called in to visit a newborn baby boy whose mother had lost six babies previously to the seven-day twitch. She had desperately wanted to make sure her seventh child lived, so she had taken a red-hot poker and burned a ring around his naval to drive away the evil spirits. When I first saw him, his belly button was a swollen, blistered mess, red and oozing. I carefully treated the burns, and checked on him several times over the next couple of days to make sure he lived past the dreaded seventh day. I also gently told the mother that burning a newborn, though done with the best intentions, would never save him.

Another time, a young peasant mother came to our house and handed me her three-pound newborn whose skin was caked with an inch of mud. I had to give him two long baths before his skin was smooth once more. In the countryside people believed that for good luck, newborns had to contact mother earth as soon as they were born. This particular rural mother was worried that her baby was listless, and therefore was probably ill, so she had covered him with more and more layers of earth. Thankfully, after the baths he became much more energetic.

Walton and I took a skinny twelve-year-old orphan into our house for the last six months of our year in Chungking. His name was Wong Ming Yu. His parents had died, and his uncle, with eight children of his own to feed, could no longer take care of him. For this reason, Wong Ming Yu had taken up residence in the field behind our house, stealing turnips from the neighbouring gardens to survive.

After noticing him shuffling back and forth behind our house, Walton and I brought him in, and made a little room for him in our attic. Wong Ming Yu was always cheerful and eager to assist us with whatever work needed doing around the house. Before long he was helping me look after Leslie and baby Murray. Eventually Walton and I sent him to the local school where he quickly made friends.

The Banquet

We lived quite happily in our little community that year, despite being slowly squeezed in the icy grip of communism. The Chinese bank would only let us withdraw fifty Canadian cents a week, in order to try and put a cap on inflation. It was barely enough to feed our family and Wong Ming Yu. I remember having to pick the bugs out of the rice we could barely afford to buy, to make it edible. You can imagine how we felt when Walton sprained his ankle on the way home one day after picking up our fifty cents weekly allowance, and had to pay sixty cents to hire someone to carry him home.

China's economy was in terrible shape at that time due to the shaky political situation after the war. At the start of that year, the ratio of Canadian dollars to Chinese Yuan was 1 to 3. By the end of the year it had changed to 1 to 3 million! Almost as quickly as paper money was printed, it was worthless. Trying to buy things at the market in those days was very stressful. Over the course of a day, the price of a sack of rice could triple. I had never seen anything like it! Communism hadn't taken over yet, but China's economy took hit after hit as the situation became increasingly heated.

One morning, Walton and I woke up to weak knocking on our door. I answered it, expecting the usual (a malnourished baby, a panicky new mother, or perhaps a scraggly orphan looking for scraps) but instead found our front porch packed with grubby nationalist soldiers, their eyes sunken, and cheekbones deeply shadowed. They had barged through the compound gate, likely scaring our poor gateman out of his wits. My fear quieted to pity. They explained that they hadn't had anything to eat or drink for days. Their general had run off with all of their wages. I invited them inside and gave them each a mug of watery tea, which was all I could afford to spare. After gratefully downing the tea, they thanked me, and were on their way, likely to beg for food elsewhere, poor souls.

Walton and I did feel that we were making good contributions in the community, being actively involved at the church and schools, and helping the local mothers and newborns. So, when the Chinese teachers and ministers held a meeting at the mission to decide what to do about the "foreigners" living in their midst, Walton and I were surprised and hurt. They came to the realization that their community would be better off coping with the Communists if they didn't have any imperialist attachments. Walton and I knew they were right, but it stung just the same. We had tried to help so many people in the neighbourhood, and now we were being asked to leave. Despite being told previously that we should pack it in with the rest of the missionaries, we had decided not to turn our backs on our friends in need, and now it was our Chinese friends who were asking us to leave. I might have been bitter, had I not seen the pain it caused them to inform us of their decision. They had little or no choice in the matter, but still it was not an easy thing to ask of us. The brutish soldiers would bully them and their families until we were gone. The more we thought about it, the more we knew that our leaving was probably for the best, for both our Chinese friends and for our young family.

Dad, meanwhile, was still living quite happily in Chengtu, where he'd met and married a wonderful Norwegian nurse named Lydia.

In 1948, the Communists had evacuated Lydia's group of Norwegian missionaries from their station. They had travelled west in a convoy, trying to keep ahead of the soldiers, and had eventually made their way to Chengtu. They were a dusty, dirty, exhausted group, looking for a place to stay.

Murray was just a newborn, and we were still living with Dad in the mission house in Chengtu, when a large truck rumbled up outside our compound. The seventeen passengers perched on top of the cargo were coated in a thick layer of sweat and dust. One of the women had the most striking blue eyes any of us had ever seen.

My father took pity on the bedraggled group and let some of them stay in his house, and some in rooms at the printing press. He was immediately drawn to blonde, blue-eyed Lydia, and would make excuses to visit her at the press to make sure she was comfortable. Of course I was asked to accompany him, so that people wouldn't suspect that something out of the ordinary was going on.

Lydia got a job working as a nurse at the tuberculosis hospital near our compound. A short time later, Walton and I were sent to Chungking and Lydia's group was told that it was now safe to return to Ankong. While she and Dad were apart, they consistently wrote letters back and forth, all the while keeping their romance a secret because of the twenty-year age difference. I remember Dad felt he had to bicycle to the post office to mail his letters to her, rather than send them with a messenger, despite the fact that his working days were packed, minute to minute. Lydia, meanwhile, had been put in charge of dropping off and picking up the mail at her clinic in Ankong, so she didn't have any problems keeping her correspondence a secret at her end.

I remember receiving letters from Dad that ended with "Lydia sends her love." Well, I hardly knew Lydia, and found it interesting that she would send her love to me. Later on I found out that Lydia had been receiving letters that ended with "Muriel sends her love."

Eventually Lydia moved back to Chengtu, where she continued her work at the TB hospital. I hadn't seen Dad with such a spring in his step since before Mother died. I knew he missed Mother very much, but it was plain to see that he was in need of companionship. It had been two and half years since Mother died. When he asked me if I would object to his proposing to Lydia, I honestly didn't. I immediately wrote a letter to Gwen and Christine in Canada, telling them how kind Lydia was, and how happy they were together. A short time later, they sent Dad their heart-felt blessings.

Lydia quickly became an important part of our family. My sisters and I knew she would never replace our mother, but she would always have a special place at the centre of our family with Dad.

Dad and Lydia didn't have any interest in leaving Chengtu, even though it was under threat of falling to communism as had happened already in other large cities in China. Neither Dad nor Lydia wanted to abandon their friends or their missionary work. I didn't like the idea of the dangers that were certain to arise once the Communists descended, knowing their strong hatred of the west. "Don't worry, Muriel," Dad assured me, "I have faith that everything will be fine."

As a family, Walton, the kids and I were unlikely to be welcomed anywhere, let alone into the United States. Before we could leave China we needed to apply for American visas because we had to pass through the States on our way home to Canada. This presented a small problem in that we had to pass a medical in order to get the visas, and we were all crawling with parasites. Walton had the usual variety of stomach worms, Leslie had hookworm and I had amoebic dysentery. I hadn't yet started showing symptoms, but found out I was sick when our failed medicals showed the results. If left untreated, I would start to suffer from severe diarrhea, weakness, cramps and weight loss. It was a sickness that affected and killed several thousand people in China every year, even though it was curable. I had probably consumed tainted water, dirty vegetables, or Chinese pickles, perhaps. I was very lucky that we caught the illness in time.

As it turned out, the solution was right under my nose. Our only healthy family member was baby Murray whose digestive system was worm-free. After collecting a sample of his stool and dividing it into four samples, I sent them off to the lab again. Shortly afterward, the lab sent us the results: four clean samples ... surprise, surprise! I sent the results off to the visa officials immediately, and a short time later, we were cleared to leave the country.

We still had our various health problems to tend to, however. Walton's worms cleared up without a problem, as the necessary medication was readily available in Chungking. Treatment for my amoebic dysentery would have to wait until we were back on Canadian soil, because the proper medication was not yet available in China. Also, I knew that the treatment would make me very sick. Leslie's hookworm, on the other hand, needed to be dealt with right away, or else it could possibly spread to her vital organs and cause all kinds of complications.

The required treatment was a capsule the size of kidney bean, filled with powerful medication. The doctor warned me that her mouth would blister if she bit down on the capsule, so it had to be swallowed whole (no easy task for a two year old). She was to ingest the medication once a day on an empty stomach, and then four hours afterwards I was to give her a dose of magnesium sulfate. Then she could have food. I planned the routine out so that I gave her the capsule at 4 a.m., then the magnesium salt at 8 a.m., so she could eat breakfast immediately afterwards. It was complicated, but nothing I couldn't manage.

A couple of days before our departure for the West, there was frantic knocking on the door in the middle of the night. It was the gateman, out of breath and flushed. He came to tell me that one of the Chinese teachers from the mission girls' school had gone into labour and was waiting by the gate to see if I could help her. I followed him down the little path from our house, and there she was—doubled over, breathing hard and clutching her belly. I knew that taking her to the hospital was out of the question. The baby was going to arrive at any moment.

The gateman and I rushed the woman up into Leslie and Murray's room. I lifted Murray from his crib, Leslie from her cot, and put them together in my bed, (Walton and I slept in twin beds down the hall from the kids' room). After my babies were more or less settled, I washed my hands and yanked up my sleeves.

Several hours into the delivery, I happened to look at my watch and see that it was 4 a.m.; time for Leslie's hookworm pill. I quickly left the red-faced woman to pant through another contraction while I carried Leslie into the living room. Usually she was so groggy at 4 a.m. that pushing the capsule to the back of her throat didn't present a problem. On that action-packed night however, Leslie had awakened to the sounds of the howling woman in the next room, and wasn't at all interested in swallowing an enormous pill. Let me tell you, two-year olds are surprisingly strong when they want to be. I actually had to ask the gateman to hold her down while I pried her little jaw apart. He grabbed at Leslie's flailing limbs, while I made another attempt to push the pill to the back of her throat. In an effort to stop me, Leslie bit down hard and burst the capsule. Immediately she started screaming as the medicine burned the inside of her mouth.

I left Leslie wailing in the arms of the gateman, whose face was beaded with sweat by this point, so I could return to the woman in labour. Only a few short moments later, the baby's head appeared.

By the time the sun came up, the children, the pregnant woman and her newborn were sleeping soundly in Leslie and Murray's room. I thanked the gateman as he slipped back to his post. Then I paused in the hallway outside the bedrooms. All was quiet and calm at last. At last!

I had my hand on the doorknob when Walton emerged.

"Good morning," he said, yawning. "What are Murray and Leslie doing in your bed?"

My finger shot to my lips to shush him. "What do you *think*?" I gestured at the room occupied by our new guests. Walton looked into the room curiously.

"Who's she? What is she doing here?" he whispered.

"For heaven's sake," I said, shaking my head. "Don't tell me you didn't hear *anything* last night!"

He shook his head, looking bewildered. "What happened?"

I sighed and told him that I was going back to sleep.

Before leaving Chungking, we tried selling some of our belongings in order to have a little extra pocket money for the long journey back to Canada. However, because of the Communists, none of our neighbours wanted items from our home. So we gave some items away, and left everything else behind. It felt very strange to walk away from a house that was full of furniture; tablecloth still carefully covering our table, with a friendly bowl of fruit placed at the centre.

Walton and I made sure that our young orphan friend, Wong Ming Yu, was well taken care of before we left. We had him admitted to the reputable orphanage in town, where we knew he would receive a good education, and left him with blankets, clothes and a mosquito net. We were confident he was in good hands there.

Despite the sticky circumstances surrounding our evacuation, the whole mission community gathered to bid us farewell with cheers and fireworks. Teachers, ministers, nurses, doctors, and neighbours all lined the sides of the road, waving and crying. The popping and hissing of the fireworks was enough to startle Murray and keep him screaming in my lap for most of the trip to the river. Walton staggered behind me with Leslie and his students who had gathered to say their goodbyes. He had come down with a fever earlier that day. His temperature was at 102 degrees. I don't know what the doctor gave him, but after his fever broke, he was as lively as a wilted rag. So there we were, a sorry bunch. I did my best to smile and wave, despite Murray's constant screams, and the nagging feeling of dread sitting like a stone in my stomach.

The airport was on an island in the Yangtze. We got there in plenty of time, but the plane took off early, leaving us behind even though we'd already paid for our tickets.

I remember there were several other families with children crammed together in the dirty, stuffy airport. It seemed like the entire place was screaming, shuffling and sweating, and we were stuck right in the middle of it. Even the walls were dripping. We didn't have anywhere to go to escape the noise, and there were no fans or air conditioners to relieve us from the insufferable heat. Walton slept most of the day, but my poor children had a terrible time. We spent an excruciating twelve hours sitting around, pacing, and fanning ourselves before we were able to board another plane bound for Hong Kong.

After we were seated and comfortable, Walton looked out the window and noticed that a gas cap on the airplane's gas tank was detached and dangling. The pilot had just started up the engine, and was preparing for take off with an open gas tank! Walton leapt out of his seat and ran to the cockpit to stop the pilot from taking off.

"The gas would have all been sucked out into the air," he muttered to me, sliding back into his seat after the engine had sputtered to a halt.

"What did they say?" I asked.

Walton grinned and shook his head. "They assured me that they weren't really ready to take off yet. Apparently they had it all under control." We watched out the window as a little man with greasy hands swiftly closed the gas cap. Walton leaned his head against the back of the seat and sighed.

We landed in Hong Kong (in one piece) after the ferryboats had stopped running from the island to mainland, so we had to recruit a little *sanpan* (row-boat) to paddle us across the harbour. Several hours later we arrived at the church guesthouse that was to be our accommodation for the night.

There were no flights to Canada the next day, nor the day after that. For ten days we waited, the four of us packed into one tiny room in the missionary residence. So many families were leaving the country at that time you could barely see the furniture for all the limbs and heads crammed into in every room of the house. On the tenth day, just when I was thinking we were fated to be left in Hong Kong, a flight to Canada became available.

By the time we finally boarded our plane out of Hong Kong, Walton and I could barely put one foot in front of the other. In fact, I don't even remember any details from that plane ride home.

When we landed in Toronto, I exhaled a long breath, and looked at Walton, my eyes reduced to slits. "I don't want to move another inch," I said, hugging Murray close to me. "Not for a long, long, time."

Chapter 7

Escaping Like a Criminal

While reading through the pile of books on China that had been collecting dust in Grandma Tonge's living room, I began to figure out China's tangled political history. I also received some help from an unlikely source: my great-grandfather, John Kitchen, who'd been dead for twenty-eight years. Grandma gave me a cassette tape of an interview with him conducted by a reporter for a local paper in Niagara Falls, Ontario, back in the 1960s. Very eloquently, he explained to the interviewer (and to me) his take on the rise of Chinese communism.

China had been politically unstable since the turn of the 20th century, when New China was born. Out with the emperors, and in with the Republic. Trouble was, no one in China really knew how to run a country. It had always been up to the emperors and generals before that. The leaders apparently appealed to the West for assistance and advice, but they were busy sorting themselves out after World War One. Meanwhile, China became over-run by warlord armies, led by power-thirsty generals, fighting each other over territories.

The first country to come to China's political and financial aid was Russia, and soon afterward, the Chinese Communist party was founded, funded and functioning. They believed it was time that China fell to the hands of China's people—the peasants and farmers— rather than corrupt generals who wanted to be treated like emperors. The Nationalist government, or Kuomintang, formed to try and rid the countryside of the warlords, and to unify the nation. The idea first came with Sun Yat-sen, who had been exiled for his extreme views by the emperor. The party grew in his absence, and was eventually led by Chiang Kai-shek. After the emperor lost his power and was dethroned, both the Nationalists and Communists sought to unify China, but only one party could be in charge. China wasn't big enough for both of them.

In the beginning, the Nationalists were more powerful than the Communists, and did all they could to keep it that way, including public executions of Communist party members.

During World War Two, the two parties united briefly to fight the warlords, followed by the Japanese who were trying to takeover the country. Eventually the Nationalists drove the Communists into the mountains where they were forced to hide from further persecution. When the atom bomb was dropped on August 9th, 1945, Japan retreated, leaving China's political parties to fight each other again. The Communists, led by their tenacious young leader Mao Tse-tung, came down from the mountains. Their strength and numbers grew exponentially, whereas the Nationalist party was bedraggled and exhausted after the war. Little money was left for defense, leaving the country wide open for a political revolution.

It was while the Communists were charging down from the north that my grandparents made their pilgrimage to Chengtu to have their second child, my uncle Murray.

Slowly but surely, while my grandparents worked in Chungking, the country fell increasingly under Communist control. Like bullies, they charged through China's cities and countryside, using violence and intimidation to take over the country, bit by bit. Having been oppressed and bullied by the Nationalist government for decades, their unleashed anger was particularly dangerous. Chengtu, because of its remote location in the far west of China, was one of the only major Chinese cities left that had not yet fallen to the Communists. But it was just a matter of time.

"Grandma, do you think you could talk about Chinese communism for a minute?" I asked, flipping the tape over in the recorder.

"Oh. What do you want to know?"

"Just a little bit about the movement. How it affected your family, that kind of thing."

She looked over my shoulder and adjusted her glasses.

"Politics has never really interested me. I have books about Communist China that people have given me, but I'm afraid I haven't read any of them. I can tell you what little I know, if it helps."

"But didn't you come in contact with them at all? You must have some stories."

"Actually, Walton and I were evacuated just before Chengtu was taken, so we were never really directly affected." Her face lit up. "But my father had quite a time!"

*

1949

Walton and I left China in September 1949, one day before the Communists took Chungking, where we'd been living. My Dad and Lydia stayed behind in Chengtu because they didn't have the heart to abandon their jobs. Dad was still the superintendent at the mission printing press, and Lydia was working at a tuberculosis hospital. Even though Lydia had recently discovered she was pregnant, she and Dad still didn't want to leave with all the other missionaries.

They stayed, Chengtu fell to the Communists, and Dad and Lydia's lives were swiftly turned upside down.

At first, Dad felt the Communist soldiers were quite civil. The people of Chengtu were able to roam the streets as they pleased, have guests in their homes, and carry on as if nothing unusual had happened.

A short time later, the authorities asked everyone who had imperialist or Nationalist connections to come forward and confess, claiming that all would be forgiven. However, if one didn't confess, and their sins against the Communist Party were later discovered, there would be serious trouble. Thousands of citizens stepped forward with their confessions.

Landowners, merchants, professors, and Nationalist soldiers all hoped for the promised forgiveness, and a clean slate in New China. Their names and addresses were entered into a large book. Several months later, all who confessed were hunted down, jailed, tortured, and even executed.

A curfew was set in place. Anyone caught outside his or her home after sundown was arrested. Soldiers were suddenly everywhere, staring people down, looking over their shoulders at every little thing. The citizens had to attend mandatory indoctrination classes, and couldn't have guests in their homes without police permission.

The Banquet

Dad and Lydia lived on the east side of the city. Many months had passed since the takeover of Chengdu, and Lydia by this point was very pregnant. Their hospital of choice was at the south end, just beyond the city walls. The total distance was about three miles, which by rickshaw would take about half an hour. When Lydia went into labour, Dad hailed two rickshaws, and then tried to make their way to the hospital. They were swiftly apprehended by the police, and told that they needed to ask permission from the local authorities before they could leave the east end of the city. Dad ran to appeal for permission, leaving Lydia to sweat and groan in the rickshaw. Finally, after swift meetings and discussions, permission was granted and they were on their way.

Next, they arrived at the south gate, where they were to exit the city to get to the hospital. Instead, they encountered more trouble. The guards at the gate said they needed permission from the city commissioner's office before they could leave. Just when they got permission, and were about to pass through the gate, they were told that their baggage had to be inspected because of the new policies in place.

Poor Lydia! And it wasn't over yet.

Having finally made their way to the hospital entrance, they were told they couldn't go inside until they'd acquired a police-written permit. After Dad finished what he hoped was his final hurdle of paperwork, they made it into the hospital, and not a moment too soon. Little Olav was born pink and healthy.

A trusted friend warned them that the Communist hospital staff had allegedly been poisoning western babies. Dad didn't want to take any risks with little Olav, so they all spent the night in a trusted doctor's house. Two days later, Dad and Lydia tried to leave, and to their dismay, found themselves facing the same obstacles on their way back to the compound. This time the guard at the south gate of the city gave them extra trouble. "You can't pass through," he grumbled.

"What's the problem?" asked Dad. "We have permission from the authorities."

"Yes, but last time you came through here there were only two of you."

"Yes?"

"Now there are three," the man said, gesturing at the little bundle in Lydia's arms.

Dad shook his head in disbelief. After lengthy explanations, the guard finally let them pass.

Along with indoctrination classes, the people of Chengtu had to attend what were called *people's courts*, which took place in open spaces throughout the city. Dad attended the first people's court in Chengtu, which was held in our church courtyard. Two men who had been minor officials under the Nationalist regime stood on a table in the middle of the courtyard. An angry mob surrounded them, hurling questions and accusations from all sides. Even small children were in attendance, to my father's disbelief. The mob shouted that the two men should be killed. Moments later, gun shots split the air, and the two men crumpled to the ground. The school children were then ordered to parade in front of the corpses, and dip their fingers in the puddles of blood. It became a mark of honour for children in Chengtu to have blood of the enemy smeared on their white school tunics.

After that day, Dad and Lydia decided that the time had come to leave China. Missionaries, with their teachings from the West, were not welcome in Red China. Also, the Communists had kicked Dad out of the printing press, and were now using the facility to print their own propaganda. In an effort to avoid trouble with Communist soldiers, many of Dad and Lydia's Chinese friends didn't want to be seen talking to westerners anymore. The atmosphere around the mission compound had soured immensely.

However, wanting to leave China, and being allowed to leave, were two very different matters. First, Dad and Lydia had to apply to the government for an exit permit, then wait six long weeks after applying before they heard anything.

Dad and Lydia were sitting in the study upstairs in their home, reading by the fireplace, when suddenly the front door flew open, and in barged two policemen. They clomped up the stairs, threw open the study door and asked for Mr. and Mrs. Kitchen.

Dad said, "That's us. What can we do for you?"

"Go to the police station tomorrow," one of the policemen said gruffly. With that, they wheeled around and let themselves out of the house.

The next day, Dad and Lydia made the trip to the police station. After answering a number of questions, they were given a list of tasks to complete before permission to leave could be granted.

First, they had to get a clearance letter from the bank of China, stating that they didn't owe anyone any money.

Second, they had to find a guarantor whom the Communists could hold responsible for Dad and Lydia's actions in Canada. For instance, if Dad was caught making derogatory comments in Canada about the

Communist government, then the Communist authorities could arrest (or torture) Dad's Chinese guarantor. Dad chose a Chinese colleague from the printing press, a trustworthy friend of the family, who had never once doubted Dad and Lydia's good nature, despite their being western.

Next, they had to place a notice in the newspaper announcing their departure. If anyone had any information that could incriminate Mr. or Mrs. Kitchen, they were to report it to the police. The notice had to appear five times in the daily newspaper, but not necessarily over five consecutive days. It could appear as often, or as seldom as the police saw fit. In Dad and Lydia's case, their notice appeared five times over a month. It was a long, grueling wait.

Finally, armed with the five published notices and having dutifully fulfilled the first and second tasks, Dad went to the police station, holding his breath. He discovered that no one had reported any complaints, so they were finally allowed to leave China. Or so it seemed.

Poor Dad and Lydia had finally reached the bus station in Chengtu and bought the tickets for Hong Kong, when suddenly Dad was tapped on the shoulder by a police officer. "You may not proceed," the man grumbled. "You must come with us back to the station."

In the brief moment before he was taken away, Dad told Lydia to take Olav to her family in Norway. He would find them there. She boarded the bus, and looked out the window as the police pulled Dad out of the transportation office. Lydia knew that westerners were being arrested and executed all over China for make-believe crimes. She held Olav tight to her chest, not knowing if she would ever see her husband again.

At the police station, Dad was pushed into a tiny, windowless room and ordered to confess to having an "imperialist" attitude. When he didn't say anything, they left him alone, telling him to think about his crimes.

Crimes? Poor Dad was so frightened and confused. He hadn't done anything wrong that he was aware of. When the policemen came back into the room an hour later, they asked him if he was ready to confess.

"Confess to what?" Dad asked.

The man grew red in the face, called Dad a string of bad names, and told him that he wouldn't be permitted to leave the station until he had confessed. He slammed the door as he left the room.

Dad closed his eyes and tried to figure out what they wanted from him.

Besides running the mission printing press, Dad had also been the treasurer of the Chengtu dental clinic. Before Chengtu fell to the Communists, Dad had been responsible for $5000 U.S. dollars donated to the mission from the United Nations. The money was to go to the dental clinic, for a new X-ray machine, and to help set up a charity fund for medical drugs needed in the hospitals throughout Chengtu. Dad went right to the bank, where he changed the U.S. dollars to Chinese silver dollars, and then loaded the bags of money into a rickshaw and took it to his office. Some of his staff helped to unload and count it, and then Dad locked the money in his safe. He withdrew funds from time to time for various purchases at the clinic, like the new X-ray machine, for example.

It dawned on Dad, as he was cooped up in the police station, that since the donation had come from a western country, the money was probably what was troubling the Communists. He opened his eyes, and peeked out the door. He asked the officer guarding the room if his arrest had anything to do with money that was donated by the United Nations.

The man grunted. "How much money did you receive?"

"Five thousand."

The officer stiffened. "Liar!" he said. "Confess the true amount."

"It *was* five thousand," Dad repeated. "Five thousand U.S. dollars. I had it exchanged to ten thousand Chinese silver dollars, which then I stored in my safe at the office."

The man's mouth twitched slightly, and his shoulders relaxed. He whispered something to another officer, and told Dad that he now had to go before the courts to receive his punishment.

After Dad was forced by the judge to pay a fine of 3000 Chinese silver dollars, Communist soldiers escorted him back to his home, and held him under house arrest. A guard was stationed at the compound gate. When Dad asked why they wanted to keep him in Chengtu, the police informed him that he was suspected of being an imperialist spy. He wasn't going anywhere.

With his ample time to pace back and forth, and try to figure out what information led to their suspicion, Dad remembered another incident. Just before the Communists had barged into Chengtu, the Foreign Bible Society of London England sent out a group of photographers and filmmakers to document the Bible society's work in China. Chengtu was the only city in China that the group was permitted to enter. Dad happened to be an agent in Chengtu for the Bible Society, so the filmmakers and photographers were sent to stay with him. Every day they went out into the city to take pictures of the gates, the people and the buildings, and make their way back to Dad's home in the evenings. They took a lot of pictures. Eventually Dad urged them to cut their trip short because the Communists were getting closer. He told the photographers that they must leave China before all the planes out of Chengtu were grounded. The group was wise enough to listen to him, and quickly made arrangements to leave.

Perhaps it was one or more of Dad's staff that had reported that he was a spy because he was hoarding imperialist funds, and he had photographers taking pictures of strategic points around Chengtu. He couldn't ever know for sure.

So there he was, cooped up alone, unable to leave his own house. Thankfully, Lin Da Neong, our amah, faithfully paid him a visit every day with food and conversation (after getting clearance from the soldiers guarding the house, of course). Communist soldiers had killed her son in a raid during the takeover of Chengtu, so she had no trouble going behind their backs and offering company to her previous employer from the West. Also, Lin Da Neong was a kind, giving person, who had been a part of Dad's family for over 30 years in Chengdu. It came as no surprise that she took such awful risks to pay her daily visits to Dad. In those dark days, she was one of his most loyal friends.

Meanwhile, the Bureau of Health and the Political Bureau were at odds over what to do with Mr. Kitchen. The TB hospital staff, since being taken over by the Communists, wanted more buildings. The house situated right next to the hospital belonged to a friend of Dad's. The Bureau of Health wanted Dad's friend to move out of his house, so that they could use the building as a part of the hospital. He said, "No problem. I'll move out, just as soon as Mr. Kitchen is allowed to leave the city. When he leaves, I'm going to move into his house." Because of this, the Health Bureau wanted Dad out of Chengtu.

Meanwhile the Political Bureau wanted to keep an eye on Dad, so they retained his papers and put him under house arrest. Why they didn't throw him into one of their jails with the rest of the political criminals was a mystery to us.

Dad passed his time worrying about how he would ever get to Hong Kong to meet Lydia and Olav. He'd received word through his network of missionary friends that Lydia had been unable to get a flight to Norway and was still waiting in Hong Kong.

After about three weeks, soldiers again showed up at his doorway, telling him that he was to go to the police station. He didn't know what they were up to, so he asked a trusted friend to accompany him to the station. Dad figured the police had dredged up some other incidents from his past in order to press more charges against him. If they were going to put him prison, then Dad wanted his friend to be there so that he could tell the appropriate people what had happened.

When they arrived at the station, the officer in charge threw Dad's passport at him, and ordered him to get out of the country within 24 hours. Dad promptly ran out of the station and purchased a bus ticket for the next day.

The next morning, Dad heard the pounding of quick footsteps on the walk outside. Dad opened the door to the grim faces of another squad of policemen. "We're looking for a man named Kitchen," said the man at the front of the pack.

"I'm Kitchen. What do you want?"

"We have reason to believe you are harbouring armaments in your well. We've come to conduct an inspection."

"Reasons to believe ... but my well was inspected last week! They didn't find anything then, and you're not going to find anything now. Go ahead and search then, it's your time wasted."

The police weren't gone for five minutes before they emerged from the well at the back of Dad's house with a shiny American Colt revolver. Brand new. It most certainly did not belong to my father. He hadn't even fired a gun in the war, let alone ever owned one. Someone definitely didn't want Dad to leave the country.

Once again, the police squad ordered Dad not to leave his house. They would be back, they said. Guards took up their posts in front of the compound gates.

Dad didn't understand why they hadn't arrested him on the spot. He suspected that they didn't have room in the jails, or perhaps they had to file reports. We'll never know, I suppose. It was lucky, in any case, that they only put him under house arrest, because this enabled his escape. So did his faithful friend, our amah, Lin Da Neong. She visited him that night, and pleaded that he try to escape the next morning before daybreak, telling him that he would likely be killed before long. Dad thought it over and decided she was right. Escaping was his only choice. He'd had enough.

So while Lin Da Neong distracted the guards at the gate, Dad ran out of the compound, under the cover of night, with only his bus ticket, a wool blanket and the clothes on his back. He ran the three miles to the bus station, escaping like a criminal, leaving his home of over thirty years.

A few hours after Dad's escape, Communist soldiers charged into the house of Lin Da Neong, demanding she tell them John Kitchen's whereabouts. Someone had directed them to her address, suggesting that she would know where he was. She had no information to give. They didn't believe her, so one of the soldiers pulled out his gun, and shot her through the heart. They left her in a crumpled heap on the floor, to be found later by her neighbours.

Dad's journey to Hong Kong rattled his nerves. He neither slept nor ate. Every time the bus stopped at a station, the police harassed him, and asked to see his papers. Sometimes they detained him, waiting for instructions from higher ranks. Fortunately for him, the communication technology was not what it is today, so the Communists couldn't keep up with him. Although the police were suspicious of him wherever he went, they didn't arrest him. He was from the West, and was in a hurry, which must have meant in their eyes that he was guilty of something. However, they never held him long enough to find out exactly what that something was. In those hectic days, there were always bigger immediate problems that needed their attention.

At last Dad made it to the footbridge of freedom that would take him to Hong Kong. He let himself be carried by the congestion and confusion as crowds of pedestrians pushed their way towards the officials guarding the entrance to the bridge. Dad looked up at the British flag that flew cheerfully at the mid-point on the bridge, and fought the lump in his throat.

However, he wasn't home free yet. Prior to Dad's escape, a missionary had been badly beaten by the guards on China's side of the bridge. They had pulled him out of the line up, suspecting he was a spy and made him walk five miles away from the bridge before he could get help. A lengthy distance, considering they had broken both his legs!

Dad wondered, as he inched towards the bridge, would they beat him too? The crowd was so dense he lost track of his own limbs. Arms and legs and heads and hats were everywhere. Slowly, pressed together like sheep, the parade of hopeful pedestrians approached the guards at the base of the bridge.

Dad's entire body thumped with his heart as he handed over his papers. The official looked him up and down, and jerked his head towards the bridge. He handed Dad his passport, and turned to inspect the next person in line.

Dad expelled a long breath, stepped up onto the bridge, and began the walk to freedom. Upon boarding a train in Hong Kong, on his way to reunite with his wife and child, Dad ordered a round of drinks for everyone in his car.

After Dad had been halted at the bus station a month earlier, Lydia experienced her fair share of adventure trying to get to Hong Kong. While Dad was being detained back in Chengtu, Lydia had been delayed in Chungking for six weeks because there weren't any planes available, and the soldiers were taking all the ships heading down river.

Finally, when there was room on one of the ships, Lydia had squeezed in among the people on the outer deck and managed to find a corner for herself and baby Olav. She had barely enough room to stand, let alone sit and breastfeed. Beside her was a man who was coughing violently and vomiting pools of dark blood—telltale signs he suffered from tuberculosis. All Lydia could do was gently ask him to face away from her and the baby while he was coughing.

She encountered more trouble when she finally reached the city of Hancow, where she had hoped to catch a bus or plane to Hong Kong. An officer approached her and wanted to know where her husband was. She told him he had been delayed. He had business.

"What type of business?"

"He has business. He's been delayed."

She answered him in this way every time he asked. Eventually the officer grew weary of her and let her go. If she had let on that her husband was in some kind of trouble, she knew they would have detained her for further questioning.

When she finally reached Hong Kong, she was able to contact one of their missionary friends, who then wrote a letter to my Dad. Lydia decided then to remain in Hong Kong and wait for Dad's arrival.

A year or so later, when Dad, Lydia and Olav had settled in Canada, Dad received a letter from Chengtu, sent by one of his Chinese friends. The friend wrote that no one in Chengtu went to church or read the Bible or cared about God anymore. He said that he no longer wanted to hear from John Kitchen, or any other missionaries for that matter. The people of Chengtu had denounced Christianity altogether.

Dad almost believed it. After reading the letter again, he spotted a smudge of a character in the bottom left corner of the page. It was small, and inconspicuous, and hadn't been interpreted by Communist officials who read all letters before allowing them to be posted. The little character at the bottom of the page said, *"Emmanuel."* God is with us.

*

Chapter 8

A Granddaughter's Quest

Muriel, Gwen, John, and Christine in Niagara Falls, Ontario. 1962. Photo by Lydia Kitchen.

*John holding Emily, with Muriel and Leslie. 1976.
Photo by Lydia Kitchen*

One crisp, fall day, Lydia was driving my great-grandfather John from their home in Niagara Falls to a missionary meeting in Toronto. They were on the freeway, driving with the flow of traffic. She was about to make a lane change to the right, when a car suddenly sped up beside her in the right lane. To avoid a collision, she overcorrected, and slammed into the car on her left. Both cars crashed into the median. John smashed his head against the windshield and was knocked unconscious. Both he and Lydia were rushed to hospital. The driver of the other car was fine, as was Lydia, but John suffered from injuries to his head and neck. He would never fully recover. My mom says that he lost his sparkle, and was just kind of blank after the accident.

I was born in 1976. When I was little more than a year old, Great-Granddad held me gently in his arms as I pooped my pants and made a big mess everywhere. Grandma scooped me up, ran upstairs and stripped me out of my soiled clothes. My mom was mortified, but Great-Granddad smiled through the whole thing.

A few months later his lungs filled with fluid as a result of complications from the car accident. He later suffocated and died in hospital.

Following John's death, Lydia lived alone in their house in Niagara Falls, spinning wool, knitting and weaving. Olav, who now works as a minister in Windsor, took good care to visit her often. He travelled with her to Chengtu in the late 1990's to see where he had been born, and where his parents, Lydia and John, had lived. On one of my visits, he and Lydia showed me videos and photographs, new and old. Lydia commented on how the development of Chengtu has changed the landscape entirely. "So many places I remember now look completely different," she said, sighing.

Before I left for China, I went to Niagara Falls to see Lydia and Olav and to look at some old photographs and maps of the Chengtu compound. When I arrived, I found Lydia reading a book that looked like it weighed more than she did: a recent biography on Mao Tse-tung. As we spoke about my travel plans, she told me in her soft Norwegian accent, her bright blue eyes sparkling, that although things had changed dramatically since she called it home, China would always have a place in her heart.

Early in the morning on March 24th, 2006, the phone rang in my little Yangshuo apartment. My mom. They usually called me at an early hour because it was the only time they could catch me, before I went to work. She called to tell me that Aunty Lydia had died of heart complications that day. She was 89.

I feel sorry that Lydia was never able to read this manuscript, but I will always be grateful for the time we spent together before I left for China.

Missionaries are no longer welcome in China, though there are several Christian congregations in many of the larger cities. Where I was living and teaching, many of the local people had no idea who Jesus was. I saw vendors selling jade crosses sold on leather string necklaces, but when I asked a Chinese friend if she knew what the symbol meant, she shrugged and said, "I don't know what it means, but I know it's a symbol from the West."

The Communists never allowed any kind of organized religion, although today they seem more and more willing to allow some degree of religious freedom in China. Christians represent a very small percentage of the population.

My ticket to working in China was not religion but my ability to speak and teach English. Just like many people of my generation, I don't consider myself to be a particularly religious person. I grew up as a member of the United Church, which I like to think of as one of the more liberal denominations within the Christian faith. As I got older, I drifted away from organized religion, hanging on only to the nostalgic traditions like Christmas Eve services.

When the Communists first began their reign over China, they were forcefully anti-western, since western countries had bullied China for centuries (forcing them into trade, and helping themselves to large chunks of China's land). This was one of the reasons why the practice of western religions had been forbidden for so many years.

Even in the early 1980's after China had begun to open up to the West, many Chinese still wanted nothing to do with westerners. My grandparents returned to China in 1982 to search for my great-grandmother Beatrice's grave, and were disheartened by the chilly reception they received. Most young people were genuinely inquisitive as usual, having not seen foreigners before and Grandma and Granddad were used to that kind of gentle curiosity. However, many people still eyed foreigners with suspicion, and gave them a wide birth.

In the thirty-odd years that have passed since then, China's feelings toward westerners have changed a great deal, at least from my perspective. When I was there, people went out of their way to be friendly and polite so that I would have a good impression of Chinese people. I found it impossible to sit in public and eat or drink alone (which, when you're travelling is a good thing). Someone always wanted to talk or make friends with me.

When I journeyed to Chengtu in search of Grandma's childhood home, I was uncertain whether or not I would have any success. Chengtu is a typical Chinese city in that it has expanded and changed a great deal since China opened up thirty years ago. The old has been torn down in favour of the new, and much of what was left behind by foreign missionaries has been replaced or redone. Since many of Grandma's friends from her childhood are either dead, or have left Chengtu and lost touch with her, I had little to go by. Because of the re-naming of so many streets, trying to find the area where she had lived was likely to be difficult in a sprawling city of four million.

I knew that close by Grandma's childhood church there had been a hospital called People's Hospital Number 2. One of my former students from Yangshuo, who had chosen the name "Snow" for his English name, found it for me on a map, and on my first day in Chengtu, he escorted me there. While walking around the grounds, we found a security guard who wanted to help us. Snow explained in Chengtu-ese that I was looking for an old street where there had once been a Canadian missionary compound. The man nodded and pointed towards the hospital exit. He told Snow that there was a church that had been built by Canadians on the street "Si Shen Ci," right around the corner from the hospital. I immediately recognized the name of the street he mentioned. I'd heard Grandma and Aunt Gwen mention Si Shen Ci many times. Grandma had been positive that by now the name of the street would have been changed. Thankfully, she turned out to be wrong!

The Banquet

John Kitchen's church in Chengtu. 2006. Photo by Emily Foster

An aerial shot of where the Canadian Missionary Compound in Chengtu would have been. The grey rooftop of one of the old mission houses can be seen nestled amongst newer buildings. 2006. Photo by Emily Foster.

My investigations in Chengtu caused word to spread quickly that there was a visiting Canadian girl trying to uncover her roots. After being in the city for only one day, a crew from the Chengtu Daily

Newspaper tracked me down, and offered to chauffeur me around the city. The story of a Canadian granddaughter travelling to China to research the childhood of her grandmother was too good a story to pass up. In China, not only is family the most important thing there is, but respecting your elders is also a deeply embedded Confucian value. The friendly folks from the Chengtu Daily helped me find the building where Grandma went to school, on the campus that had been built by Canadian missionaries, and then wrote a feature story about it, complete with pictures. After four days of articles about my adventures in Chengtu, I heard a customer in a convenience store refer to me in Chinese as "that Canadian girl" to her husband. Everywhere I went, people smiled warmly, asked and answered questions, and tried their best to make me feel at home.

While poking around, I wanted to see if there was still a population of Chinese Christians in Chengtu. The ministers whose names I'd been given were out of town, or busy, but were able to tell me over the phone that their congregations were full every Sunday. They estimated the Christian population in Chengtu to be around 5000 people.

As we explored the street where my grandma grew up, I led Snow away from People's Hospital No. 2, until we were standing in front of a large church, topped by a bright red cross on the roof. "This is it!" I said, looking up at the large stained glass window looking out at the street. Here was the church where John Kitchen was the minister during his 31 years in Chengtu. According to the woman who was sweeping the steps when Snow and I arrived, the church still boasts a full house every Sunday.

I wanted to get a look inside to see if any of my great-grandmother Beatrice's paintings were still displayed, or if the plaque dedicated to her after the plane crash had been returned to its place on the back wall. During the Cultural Revolution in the 1960's, a member of the church congregation had taken the plaque, believing it was in danger of being stolen and/or destroyed. The woman standing at the door of the church felt quite strongly that I shouldn't be allowed to roam around inside the church. Snow explained that I was the great-granddaughter of one of the first ministers at that very church. He promised that we would be very quick and respectful. She deliberated on it for a long time, looking around as if she was afraid a bolt of lightning was going to strike her at any minute. Finally, she stepped aside, and let us in. "But no pictures," she warned, shaking a finger at the camera in my hand.

I found nothing. No paintings, or stained glass, or any plaques of any kind on the walls. It was quite dark and dramatic, as churches tend to be, its high ceiling, criss-crossed with new wooden beams, (installed after the previous roof had been destroyed by Japanese bombs). I pleaded with the woman to let me take one picture, for my grandmother. "It would make her so happy, to see her childhood church," I said. She gave me a shaky smile, then waved the go-ahead. But I had to be quick, and then I had to get out.

Having found the church, I knew the mission houses had to be close by. Walking around the perimeter of what looked like a walled-in housing community across the street from the church, Snow and I came across a smiling elderly man who was curious about me. Why was I walking around his street with a camera? What was I looking for? When he discovered I was *Jia-na-da ren* (Canadian), his eyes grew very big, and he began gesturing at the looming grey house behind him. He explained to my student in their local dialect that he'd been living in that area all of his 84 years, and he knew which houses had been built by Canadians. He introduced himself as Mr. Li.

"He wants to show us," Snow told me, gesturing excitedly. "We have to follow him."

The walled-in community was a maze of red brick walls, and tucked-away doorways. Walking down the cramped alleyway between the many residences, suddenly Mr. Li pointed up to an old grey building with large windows and a dusty roof. "Jia Na Da ren," I heard him say. Canadians.

The old mission houses were easy to spot, their angular roofs poking up above the blocky brick housing that had been built in every available space since Chengtu's population had exploded. Four of the Canadian houses remained. They stuck out like large grey boulders amongst blocky brick apartments.

Mr. Li led us inside the front doorway of the first Canadian building we came to. Inside it was dark and musty. I counted a dozen electrical meters in the windowless foyer, their numbers glowing red on the wall. What was once a single-family home is now divided up to house twelve families!

When I called later on to tell her breathlessly what I had seen, Grandma explained that the missionary houses were large in an attempt to keep the rooms cool in the times before fans or air conditioners.

The wooden floors creaked as we ascended the well-worn staircase. All the doors on the second floor were closed and locked. Everything, even the light slanting through the grime-streaked window, looked old and tired.

Mr. Li took us around to each of the four Canadian buildings that remained. I tried to navigate my way around but the alleyways turned every which way like a maze. Every old courtyard, backyard and porch from the old compound had been crammed with housing.

While exploring the hallways and porch of the fourth Canadian house on our tour, Mr. Li pointed out the yellow apartment building pushed up against the small backyard below us, and explained that an old Canadian building used to be there but had been torn down. "Your great-grandfather spent a lot of time there."

Unfortunately "printing press" didn't translate very well, but Mr. Li, who could actually recall my great-grandfather John Kitchen, thought it had been the place where he had worked. I found out later that the printing press had gradually gone bankrupt, and had been torn down only five years earlier. I probably would never have known the significance of that shabby yellow apartment building, if it hadn't been for my friend, Mr. Li. And Snow, of course.

I realized, after Mr. Li pointed out where the printing press would have been, that Grandma's house would have been the one closest to it, because her father was the press supervisor. I looked around me again, at the dusty porch floor, the sinking roof above me, and the little green square of yard below. I was standing in Grandma's house!

I inspected a nearby door jamb, where there was enough space to hide foreign coins from inspecting Communist officials, and thought of my great-grandfather, holed up in that house for 3 weeks alone. I poked my head up a set of spooky stairs that appeared to have been closed off, and thought of my grandma and her sisters running up and down the hallways, chasing each other. Looking out at the little yard, I imagined their big butterfly kites flying up over the compound wall, 76 years ago.

*

Chapter 9

Hong Kong: A New Start

"How was your Dad when he returned to Canada after escaping from China?" I asked Grandma, shifting in the plastic deck chair.
She sighed. "He was jittery. He didn't talk about what happened very often."
"Did he still have a good sense of humour, at least?"
"Oh yes. But he was sad. He missed the old China. Dad suffered slight brain damage after he and Lydia were in that car accident. He was never really the same after that."
Just then one of Grandma's neighbours laughed in his yard. Grandma turned her head to look. I put my hand on her arm to focus her attention back to me.
"What about you? Did you miss China once you were back here?"
"Oh yes, terribly."

1950

As happy as I was to be back in Canada, I thought about China all the time. I wasn't sure if we would ever get to work there again because we had to wait to be invited back, and that wasn't likely as long as the Communists were in power. I wasn't in any position to get my hopes up. Walton and I were certain that we were in Canada to stay.

In 1951, our son David was born. We were living in the rural town of Lakefield, Ontario at the time. Life was straightforward and happy, with lots of socializing with neighbours and our church congregation. It was a great time for our young family. After a few years, all my dreams of returning home to China had withered.

Walton was the minister in town. I was the minister's wife, a homemaker for the first time. When we first moved to Lakefield, we had very few belongings, as most of our furniture and clothing had been left behind in Chungking. At that time, Walton was making $2300 a year, which was under $200 a month. Half of his salary had to go into the purchase of a family car, so every month we found ourselves sinking deeper and deeper into debt.

Thankfully, the good folks in our congregation took great care of us. Many donated furniture, clothing, and home-cooked meals now and then. One man in particular stepped up and helped out in ways that baffle me to this day. His name was Dr. Renwick, a kindly older gentleman. He took a liking to our family right away. He was a dentist, but also bought and sold property as an investment and hobby. At the time, he owned a large plot of land on Lake Chandos, up in central Ontario's cottage country. He tried to convince Walton to buy a piece of the lake frontage at $100 for 100 feet, which worked out to be a very reasonable $1 per foot. However, it was still more than we could afford at the time. Once again, our family was living with the very basics, and a plot of land in cottage country was not something we needed.

A short time after Walton turned down the offer, Dr. Renwick approached him again, beaming. "My son tells me that you own a Leika camera! Is this true?"

Walton nodded. It was the one he'd bought in Shanghai, for $20. We had carted that camera all over China with us, and had brought it back to Canada.

Dr. Renwick smiled, and gave Walton a pat on the shoulder. "How about a trade? I'll give you land, if you give me that Leika. What do you think?"

How could such an offer be refused? Eventually, Dr. Renwick had a summer cottage built for us on the land. It took us five years to pay him back, interest free. All of the cottage furniture came from donations from our congregation. Our family cottage was christened with the name "Tien Men," which means "Gateway to Heaven." Tien Men was also the name of the town where Mother's plane went down.

Eventually, after we'd paid off our car, we were able to work our way out of debt, and began to relax and enjoy our cottage and home in Lakefield.

I never stopped thinking about China, though. Walton and I always worried about our Chinese friends, who were struggling under the Communist regime. They had stopped writing to us, for fear of getting into trouble with the authorities, so we lost touch for a while. Walton and I knew that China was troubled, but because the Communists had cut the country off from the rest of the world, we had no idea what was going on, and there was no way to find out.

Our daughter Elizabeth, born in 1957, was just a few months old when we were invited by the Church of Christ in China to work in Hong Kong. The Chinese Christian University of Chung Chi needed a chaplain, and Walton was perfect for the job. Chung Chi means, "Reverence for Christ" and was founded by professors from various Christian colleges in China who fled to Hong Kong when the Communists took over. Hong Kong then was still a colony of Britain.

We accepted without hesitation, and made the necessary preparations to depart. In 1957, Leslie was ten, Murray was eight, David was six, and Elizabeth, a newborn. It was a lot of work, uprooting our young family, but we knew the experience of living in Asia would be as valuable for our kids, as it had been for my sisters and me.

We lived on the island of Hong Kong for one year in order to study Cantonese, which is the prevalent language in Hong Kong. After a year we were sent out into the New Territories, which is the large outer section of the mainland. Hong Kong consisted of the island of Victoria, a large section on the mainland called Kowloon city, and the New Territories. Chung Chi College, where Walton was the chaplain, was located twelve miles into the New Territories. We lived out in the sticks, as our kids liked to say. For the first time in my life as a missionary, we didn't live in a compound, but in a flat on campus, together with the university staff and students.

One might assume that my four kids enjoyed an exotic upbringing, living and going to school in Hong Kong, but they would tell you that it was just living. They had friends from all over the world, and their friends—as is the case for young people everywhere— meant everything to them. If our kids weren't bringing their friends home from school with them, then they were going to their friends' houses.

We didn't have television, and neither did any of our friends, so my children learned to entertain themselves when they weren't working on their studies. They spent hours hiking, playing at the beach, touring around in our little motor boat, swimming at a nearby waterfall, playing sports, or going to the YMCA to watch films.

Elizabeth, being too young for school when we first moved to Chung Chi, was the only one of our four kids to pick up Cantonese. She played with local children, not just the other missionary kids. She always had a grubby entourage of friends keeping her company while her siblings were away at school.

I remember a time when I'd made Elizabeth a beautiful green sundress for the opening of the Chapel at Chung Chi. All of our children looked wonderful before we left for the service. They were smiling, clean and smartly dressed. Walton and I arrived at the church early, to meet and greet the guests. Our children came a short time later. It wasn't until after the service, when we gathered for a picture with the group of United Church missionaries and the bishop of Hong Kong, that I noticed my four year old was no longer wearing the lovely sundress I'd made her specially for the occasion. Instead, she had on an old red sweater with a broken zipper, and a pair of ripped corduroy pants.

Elizabeth saw me barreling towards her, red-faced. She stood up straight, stuck out her little chest and said, "Mommy, next time you give me new clothes, you have to give my friends new clothes too." She pointed at the row of dirt-smudged faces, watching us from the side of the chapel. Honestly, what could I say to that?

During the summer vacations, Walton and I liked to take the kids out of Hong Kong to see more of the world, and to get away from the city heat. We went to Japan one summer, and Malaysia another, but the place we visited most was a camp of sorts at the top of Lan Tau island. There were no trees up there, only scraggly bushes. A dammed up stream made a fine swimming hole for the kids. We had a little cabin there, a squat stone building with hefty shutters, low ceilings and very basic amenities. The huts had been built to withstand the typhoons, you see. They were sturdy, damp, and not all that homey, but at least they were cool and comfortable. We ate in a common mess hall, with twenty or thirty other families. Our kids always made friends and found ways to entertain each other.

David in front of our summer retreat on Lan Tau island. 1960.
Photo by Muriel Tonge

The Banquet

The Tonge Family: Murray, Walton, Leslie, Elizabeth, Muriel, David. 1963

View from the Tonge apartment of Tolo Harbour and Chung Chi College playing field. 1960. Photo by Muriel Tonge.

Jellyfish were a part of life in Tolo Harbour, where the kids would swim when we lived at Chung Chi. One spring there was a strange phenomenon in the harbour; for some reason, thousands more jellyfish had been born than normal, and they had clogged up the water. It was like trying to swim in tapioca pudding! The baby jellyfish were too young to have stingers yet, thank goodness, so our kids developed a game similar to a snowball fight, lobbing baby jellyfish back and forth at each other.

Thankfully, despite oddities like jellyfish fights, growing up in Hong Kong was normal and every-day to our kids. After all is said and done, that's all you can ask for in a childhood. As for me, I never experienced a dull moment in Hong Kong. Besides looking after our children, hosting dinner parties and running our household, I was also a volunteer residential nurse for Chung Chi College, which kept me busy.

One day, a sweaty young woman ran to our flat, (we did not yet have telephones) to summon me to the girl's residence where a student was vomiting violently and had severe diarrhea. In those early days the college didn't have a clinic or any kind of medical care staff except me. So I left in a puff of dust to visit the sick student.

That year there had been a surplus of pork in Canada. The Canadian government bought the pork to keep the farmers from losing too much money, and had it tinned and sent off to charitable institutions.

We requested hundreds of cases of the Canadian tinned pork for the students and staff at Chung Chi College. Unfortunately, it was summer at the time, and the tins of pork required refrigeration once opened, but there were no instructions or warnings printed on the label. No one had refrigerators in the poor communities in those days, so hungry students who rationed their opened tins of pork, regretted it terribly, and the calls came pouring into the health clinic.

I had never seen such an outbreak of food poisoning in all my life. The ambulance became a shuttle between the college and the hospital. I tried to treat as many people on site as I could, but was quickly overwhelmed. It seemed like every room in every residence on campus emitted sour vomit smells, and pitiful cries for help. All day and night I ran from room to room with my little medical kit. Just as things would slow down in one area, I'd have to run off to another part of the campus. I was running around for three days straight. Luckily things calmed down after a week or so, or else I don't know what we would have done.

On another occasion, a parcel arrived at our flat that would forever change my life. A church in Canada had sent a large box of pastel-coloured baby clothes. I'd heard of an Anglican orphanage two miles up the road called St. Christopher's, so I decided to pay them a visit, taking the parcel with me.

St. Christopher's was a cluster of cottages built into the hillside. Each cottage housed about sixteen children, aged six to eighteen, plus a housemother or housefather. The boys were taught agriculture, building and handyman skills while the girls were taught housekeeping and sewing. A nearby Lutheran Bible college, made up of two large buildings, had been turned over to St. Christopher's and became a baby home. Former girls of the orphanage, who hardly knew one end of a baby from the other, were taking care of as many as sixteen babies. Every baby had gastroenteritis, which gets extremely messy, and there wasn't a single diaper to be found anywhere. I looked. Instead, the girls were using filthy rags and parts of old denim jeans, but couldn't keep up with the continuous mess. You can imagine the smell, I'm sure! On top of everything else, most of the babies were suffering from infected prickly heat, which looks like a red rash dripping with pus. Perspiring constantly, and not getting proper cleaning usually results in prickly heat. It broke my heart.

In Hong Kong, people called me Tonge Tai, a short form for Tonge Tai Tai. (The family name always precedes the given name in China, as you know.) Tai Tai means, "wife of a learned man." I knew I was going to have to stretch beyond being the wife of a learned man, however, while living in Hong Kong. That day at St. Christopher's, I found my mission.

Bishop Hall, the Anglican Church figure of authority, had been living and working in Hong Kong for thirty years. The Anglicans had been sending missionaries to Hong Kong and China since the turn of the century. This meant that Bishop Hall had to have his hand in everything to do with St. Christopher's because it was an Anglican-run facility. I wasn't Anglican, but I cared deeply about what they were accomplishing at the orphanage, and that was all that mattered. As missionaries, we were ultimately working for the same cause, so it didn't matter from which denomination of the church you came. We all just wanted to help people where we could.

Shortly after writing Bishop Hall a testy letter about the state of his St. Christopher's Baby Home, I received a call from him asking me to take over as the Baby Home supervisor. That was it. At last my course was set!

As the wife of a missionary, my services were free, which I didn't mind because it meant that I could do what I wanted, and didn't have to worry about being bossed around by anyone. If I didn't like what people were doing, I could give them a piece of my mind, without fear of losing my job. My only concern at St. Christopher's was the welfare of the babies.

Despite being delighted with my newfound sense of purpose, the responsibility terrified me. I wanted to impose changes, and I knew I would have to appeal to people for money and help. Although I was intimidated at first by the mountain of work that needed to be done, on my first day of work, I rolled up my sleeves, and got down to it.

First, I went to a local towel factory and bought one hundred cheap towels to use as diapers. My next order of business was to get a hold of more money. Thankfully, I didn't have to wait long. After sending a letter of appeal to the United Church in Canada, clothing, diapers and money began to arrive. I made friends with a carpenter in town who made toddler chairs and cribs. After several months passed, he couldn't make them fast enough to keep up with our demand. Babies gathered at our doorstep like leaves in a gutter. One after the other they filled every available space. I had two babies per crib, babies in boxes and dresser drawers. They were multiplying before our very eyes!

At that time, people were pouring over the border from China into Hong Kong, seeking refuge from the Communists. Thousands of squatter shacks made from discarded wood and cardboard dotted the hillsides and lined the streets. Some poor souls even took up shelter under stairwells. More and more Chinese refugees arrived every day, many of them members of what once was the middle-upper class: doctors, professors, teachers, dentists. They were reluctant to ask for help once they got into Hong Kong for fear of being sent back to China.

When mothers without money gave birth to babies, sometimes abandoning the baby was the only option. Usually parents left these babies in visible, safe places, where they would be found quickly. I know of many cases where mothers went to the hospital in labour, gave a false name and address, gave birth, and then slipped away into the night. Babies were left in waiting rooms, market places, and even movie houses. On average, one baby was abandoned per day in Hong Kong. When someone discovered an abandoned baby, the police would be called, the baby would be picked up, and then taken to one of the overflowing orphanages in the area.

You can imagine my contempt when the Medical Officer of Health arrived to inspect our Baby Home, and gruffly informed me that the babies' heads were to be six feet apart, or with a glass partition between them, by law. I recall laughing and saying, "Funny man." The law, as in many places in Hong Kong, could not always apply at St. Christopher's Baby Home.

From Monday to Friday, Leslie, Murray and David left for school at 7:30 a.m. and took a train from the New Territories to the British schools in Kowloon. They did not return until 5:30, which gave me a full working day at St. Christopher's. Elizabeth would come with me to work, and play with the other toddlers. On a couple of occasions, people who were visiting the home in the hopes of adopting showed an interest in Elizabeth. I had to explain that no, she hadn't been abandoned. She was always a little scruffy-looking, wearing her brother's hand-me-downs, playing outside with the other children. She was far from abandoned!

In a matter of months, our baby home had grown from 16 to 130 babies! It was impossible for me to turn babies away, even though we were over capacity, but money from the Anglican church in Hong Kong, and the Canadian and American Sunday schools helped out a great deal.

At this point we had two buildings for the babies and the live-in caregivers. One building had two stories of dormitories, with rooms for the staff. The second building had probably housed the Bible College offices and lecture halls. The rooms were large enough to hold classes of fifty students or more. We redesigned these rooms for the babies. One room, painted blue, was for the babies six to twelve months old. Another large room we painted pink, and used for the tiny infants. Slowly but surely, the money trickled in, and we were able to provide more cribs, blankets, diapers, food and medicine.

One day I was sitting in the isolation room feeding a tiny new infant with a gastric tube. I looked up and jumped. A giant of a man standing at the door watching me smiled sheepishly and apologized for the fright. He asked me for a tour of the facilities. This type of visitor was common, and usually welcome, because once people saw what kind of outfit we ran they were willing to offer funds. This man was no exception. In fact, after we had completed our tour, he turned to me and asked, "Muriel, what do you think you need for this place? Just name it."

I laughed and shook my head. "Everything, and anything," I said. "From stools, blankets, to ... well ... we could really use a new building."

He nodded thoughtfully. As it turned out, this gentle giant was the man in charge of the World Refugee Funds. He made up his mind right then and there to help us get the money for a brand new building we so desperately needed!

Bishop Hall needed to be contacted before anything could go forward, which was a challenging task, as he was all but impossible to get a hold of. Telephone calls led to disgruntled secretaries who informed me that the Bishop would get back to me as soon as possible, which I knew, from experience, would never happen. He was a man much in demand. This time I knew I would have to take drastic measures to get a word with him. I wanted that new building.

Bishop Hall lived close to our home in the New Territories. I did a little private investigating and found out what time he left his home to go work. So, the next day I was at the gate to meet him as he left his compound, my thumb sticking out, a broad smile on my face. He picked me up, and I found myself with forty-five minutes of his undivided attention. I explained why we needed a new building at the baby home, and how we just *had* to accept the generous offer from the World Refugee Fund. It didn't take much for Bishop Hall to agree. Before long, he was as excited as I was.

St. Christopher's orphanage. 1960.

Muriel and a helper with the babies. 1961

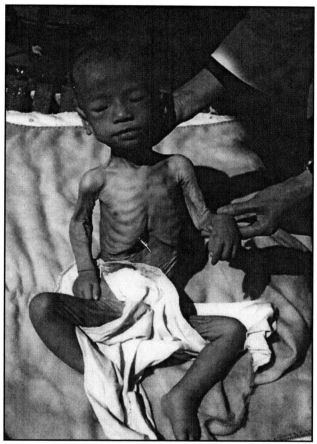

One of many abandoned babies brought to St. Christopher's Home. 1960. Photo by Muriel Tonge.

It took two years to finish the building, due to construction problems and constant delays. In the meantime, donations kept pouring in. One stifling day we got a visit from two sweating Hollywood actors, William Holden and Peter O'Toole. At the conclusion of their tour, they purchased two air conditioners for us, which we promptly installed in the blue and pink rooms. We were getting inundated with clothing, bedding and equipment by this time from global charity and church organizations around the world. We eventually became so well stocked that we started sending clothes and diapers to other baby centers around Hong Kong.

When a baby came under our care at St. Christopher's, I would give him or her a name and approximate birth date, and then apply for a birth certificate. We had a month to try and find the biological parents before the baby became a ward of the government. Next there were five months of putting ads in the papers, trying to track down the rightful parents, just in case there had been a mistake, or the parents had changed their minds. If no one came forward then the baby was put up for adoption.

Chinese and western families adopted many lucky children as well. Seeing a baby go from starving to smiling, on their way to a new home, is a sight unlike any other. That was what kept me going day after day.

The Baby Who Never Smiled

One day the police brought us an abandoned little boy. They calculated he was about seven months old, but after giving him an examination, and seeing that he had a full set of upper and lower teeth, I knew he was almost two years old. He weighed barely eleven pounds, couldn't sit up on his own, and had very little hair, which added to his infantile appearance. His skin was dry and scaly, almost like parchment, which made me suspect that he was a river-baby and had been born on a boat, exposed to lots of sun and salt water. He never smiled. We tried and tried, by holding him, ticking him, making silly faces and noises at him, and still the tiny boy would never smile. I named him Jamie.

After several weeks of working with Jamie, trying to clear up his prickly heat and get him to gain some weight, I earned his trust. After a few more weeks, he loved to sit on my hip, his wiry arms and legs wrapped around my torso. I would go about my daily business, with Jamie clinging to me like a bony accessory.

One day some visitors arrived to have a look at some of the orphans. Jamie was asleep with his little head nestled into my neck. A dribble of pus trickled from an infected pustule on his head and dripped onto my neck. One of the visitors asked, "Aren't you worried that you might ... catch something from him?"

I shook my head and held Jamie closer to me.

After taking him to the hospital to get X-rays, we found out that Jamie had tuberculosis and pleurisy (a lung disease that isn't around much anymore). Although we had successfully cleared up his prickly heat and gastroenteritis he was sent away to a hospital for four months so they could take care of his TB.

When Jamie returned from the hospital, he was better, but wasn't one hundred percent yet. About a year later, he had gained weight, and even wore a smile on his face. A missionary couple from our mission came in one day and asked if they could take him home with them, just for the weekend. They wanted a trial run, so to speak. He was three years old by this time. I agreed, knowing and trusting the couple completely. When Sunday rolled around, the woman showed up with Jamie in her arms, and thrust him at me. "Take him," she said, turning away to keep me from seeing her trembling lip. I ran after her to find out what was wrong, and heard her muttering, "We have to have him, Muriel. We just *have* to have him."

A short time later, her wish came true. Because she was a nurse, and Jamie still required special care because of his tuberculosis, it was a practical and perfect match.

Jamie grew up happily with his adoptive parents who continued to work in Hong Kong. Over the years, I would visit them, and would remind Jamie, with a gentle poke to the belly, that he would always be a little bit mine.

He now lives in Calgary with his wife and children, and works as a chartered accountant. I still get Christmas cards from him and his family every year. Jamie grew up to be a lovely person, with a warm and wonderful smile.

Calling Dr. Tonge

One week we had a terrible scare. High fevers were tearing through the Home. A tiny one-year-old baby was sent to the hospital when his temperature reached 106 degrees, which is dangerously high for infants. Later on we got a call from the hospital telling us that the baby had died after his temperature had soared to 109! Another baby died in the Home, not long after that, with a temperature of 108. Then two more babies came down with temperatures of 107. I was terrified that whatever was causing the fevers would spread throughout the entire home, killing all the babies one by one.

None of our regular doctors were available at the time of the fever outbreak, but I needed to have tests done immediately. I needed a doctor to complete the necessary paperwork. One doctor from the local clinic was sick, another was in court for something or other, and a third could not leave his clinic to come to St. Christopher's. None of my doctor friends could come either, for reasons that escape me now. In any case, I was strapped.

There was only one thing I could think to do. I took stool samples from the babies with fevers and sent them to the government hospital in the city and signed my name as Dr. Tonge. Sure enough, the results came back to me in no time. The babies had staphylococcus infections. So Dr. Tonge ordered the necessary medication, isolated the sick babies, and soon enough the infection was all cleared up.

The government officials were none the wiser.

Typhoon

I received a panicky call from one of the live-in caretakers at the Home one night, shortly after the area had been ravaged by a violent typhoon. Our house at Chung Chi was relatively sheltered from the wind and rain, so I had no idea of the storm's severity.

The new building for the Baby Home had been built on the edge of a large hill, which was lovely for the hot days when the breeze swept through the windows. Unfortunately, the building was right in the pathway of the typhoon.

This particular storm hit the harbour and the Baby Home hard. I remember seeing dozens of fishing boats splintered on the rocks on my way to work. I arrived at the Home as the rain was subsiding and the sun was coming out. Every window on the south side of the building was broken, and the nurseries were flooded with two inches of water. The night staff had moved all of the beds and cribs to the other side of the room, away from the broken windows. One of the big tables we used for changing diapers had toppled over. All of the babies, toddlers and even the live-in staff were wailing. The tiniest babies had been fed, but there was no food for the toddlers and caregivers.

I found the kitchen staff huddled together, hiding and whimpering in the inner pantry. The older children from the orphanage came to help us clean everything up and tend to the little ones.

Besides the physical destruction, the typhoon left us without electricity or water for ten days! We didn't have disposable diapers in those days, so all of the diapers had to be hand-washed by our staff. We were dependent on our running water. Then there was the problem of food for the toddlers. We used an electric food processor to puree vegetables and meat into thick gruel for baby food, but we were stuck without electricity! We would have to mash the food up by hand—a daunting task when there were more than one hundred mouths to feed!

I telephoned a nearby British Army camp, and told them how we had been affected by the typhoon. In the past, when women from the camp had come by to ask if we needed assistance, I'd said, "Don't ask unless you are really serious about helping, because we can always use assistance."

The kind women organized a system for dealing with our heaping pile of dirty laundry. They became our very own diaper service, taking away the dirty and bringing back the clean. I don't know what we would have done without them!

As for the food situation, we received aid from agencies such as C.A.R.E. (Cooperative for Assistance and Relief Everywhere), Red Cross, Mennonite World Service, and Church World Service, who had heard of our plight. I filled out forms for each organization, checking off whatever they were offering such as sugar, biscuits, powdered milk and soap.

On one occasion, I was too busy to fill out the details on the C.A.R.E. supply request, so I wrote, "Send us anything you have." Well, "anything" turned out to be instant tea, bottles of perfume, and the stuff used to hold dentures in place! I'm sure we somehow managed to put it all to good use somehow!

One Catholic agency told me they were teaching a course in noodle making, and asked if we would like some noodles. I requested five hundred pounds of noodles per month (a number I pulled out of my head). It seems like a lot of noodles, but remember we needed food for the whole orphanage, including sixty-five staff! One hundred and sixty children from age three to eighteen lived at St. Christopher's, plus 120 babies and toddlers. We were given noodles every month for half a year, at no charge.

I really don't know what we would have done without the kindness of those charitable organizations. My faith in humanity soared through the roof in those difficult times. Even typhoon clouds have silver linings now and then.

The Trouble with Tainted Water

At 9 p.m. one night I received an urgent call from the Baby Home. It seemed there was a strong kerosene smell coming from the tap water. The problem was that the water had already been used to make formula, and twenty babies in the blue room had already been fed.

Mrs. Chu, my assistant, had phoned the clinic, and had been told that all twenty babies needed to be brought in to have their stomachs pumped immediately. Poor Mrs. Chu's voice quivered as she explained the situation to me over the phone.

"Just wait," I told her calmly. "Let me make some phone calls first and I'll get back to you."

I called three other doctor friends of mine. Two told me to sit tight and keep the babies under close observation overnight. The third doctor advised stomach pumping.

It was 10 p.m. by this time, and I knew Mrs. Chu was probably at her wit's end. Taking all twenty babies into the clinic would save their lives, but loading the babies into tubs and putting the tubs into the Home's station wagon would also be an immense undertaking. We also worried that having their stomachs pumped would traumatize the poor little things.

After much hand wringing and pacing, I called Mrs. Chu and asked for a report on the babies. She said they were sleeping soundly. I told her to keep a close eye on them, and report back to me in two hours.

I didn't sleep much that night, but thankfully, the babies did. They recovered just fine.

So, where had the kerosene smell come from? Well, the water for the Baby Home and the rest of the orphanage came from a mountain stream, which also supplied water to a nearby village. It was springtime, and the farmers were flooding their rice fields. After doing a little investigating, I discovered that some of the farmers had needed more water. One evening, they went up and using rags, had partially plugged some of the pipes that ran down to our orphanage in order to divert the water to their fields. The rags they used had previously been used to wipe up kerosene.

The farmers never made that mistake again after I was through with them, let me tell you!

Poisonous Allegations

One day a request came in from the Presbyterian Casework Centre to come and pick up a baby. He was a fat six-month-old whose parents lived in a stairwell with their four other children. His father was sickly and couldn't get any work. His mother was a cleaning lady but wasn't making enough money to support the family. The Presbyterian Casework Centre gave them rice, clothing, and paid their education fees, but the family still couldn't manage a fifth child.

I told them that they had to go to the government agency to sign adoption papers before we could take their baby. The following week they called us, saying the papers were signed, and the baby was waiting for me at the Casework Centre.

It was a Friday. I don't remember why Leslie was with me instead of being at school that day, but in any case, I brought her along with me to hold the baby while I drove. We got to the centre at 4:30 so most of the employees had already left, save one caseworker. I asked to see the adoption papers, and she informed me that they hadn't arrived yet, but it was all right for me to take the child. What else was I to do? The Centre would be closed for the weekend, and the caseworker certainly wasn't going to take him to her home. He had nowhere else to go.

I didn't like it. Something didn't feel right, but I took him back to the Home with me, anyway.

Wouldn't you know it, the next day I got an urgent call from a government official! "Mrs. Tonge," he said slowly, "whatever you do, *don't* take the cleaning lady's baby."

"Why not?" I asked, feeling blood drain from my face.

"The parents have set us up. They want us to pay $400 for him. If you take him, they can charge us."

I pressed my hand against my forehead and sighed.

"Mrs. Tonge?"

"I have the baby. I brought him here last night. I didn't know what else to do."

The government official sighed then cleared his throat. "Don't worry about it. We'll figure something out," he said.

A day or two later I was told that the Casework Centre didn't want the baby to go back to his family. They had learned that the father had tuberculosis, and that he and his wife were trying to pay for medicine by selling their baby!

One night the baby boy developed a slight temperature. It wasn't anything to be concerned about, but I was already uneasy about having him at the Home. I didn't want any more excitement. I took him to the Tai Po clinic to see my friend Dr. Perry. He couldn't find anything wrong, so I brought the baby back to St. Christopher's, and left him in the care of the night shift.

A phone call woke me up in the early hours of the morning. One of the night shift caregivers at the Home told me tearfully that the cleaning lady's baby had died in the night.

Shortly after word spread that he had died under my care, a police officer informed me that the parents were accusing me of poisoning the baby. I was instructed to meet the parents and a detective at the morgue at 9 a.m. sharp. When I arrived, the parents hollered at me, calling me a murderer and a demon woman. They threw accusations this way and that, without shedding one tear for their deceased son.

When we went in to look at the baby's corpse, his blood had pooled and sunk in such a way that his stiff little body was covered in black and blue markings. Now his parents claimed I had beaten *and* poisoned their son.

Thankfully I was known in the community as a good person. Dr. Perry told the coroner and the detectives that I could never do something so horrible. His word was respected apparently because the coroner ended up asking me to help him write his report, as the cause of death was a mystery. I told him that I suspected the baby had suffered from a heart condition, which was why the fever had killed him.

When we left the morgue, the place was crawling with reporters. One of the caseworkers from the Presbyterian casework centre stepped out of the crowd with a letter from the baby's parents demanding 400 Hong Kong dollars for their son. Suddenly the detective turned on the parents, realizing what kind of people they were, and the case against me was suddenly dropped.

However, the Communist newspapers picked up the story, and printed that a white American nurse had killed an innocent Chinese baby. They alleged that I ripped the screaming baby from the arms of the crying mother and refused to give him back.

Naturally Bishop Hall wanted to know what had really happened. I told and retold my story to the Bishop, to government officials, to friends and neighbours. I had nothing to be afraid of, as far as I knew. My only crime was taking the baby before seeing the adoption papers. I would never make that mistake again.

Thankfully, as quickly as the storm hit, it subsided. The Hong Kong government threatened to send the couple back to China if they continued with their accusations. The father, having worked as a Nationalist army officer, couldn't let that happen, so they kept their mouths shut and continued to accept handouts from the Presbyterian Casework Centre without malice. I was left alone.

The Tough Side of Tonge Tai

Kwung Wah was a free of charge Buddhist charity hospital in Hong Kong that promised never to turn anyone away. I visited the maternity ward many times, and was disgusted to see two women in each bed. Can you imagine being pregnant in a single bed beside another woman in labour? Patients were sprawled on the floor and in the hallways. It was better than nothing, I suppose, but I would send babies there only as a last resort. Usually the children came to us from Kwung Wah when the hospital ran out of room.

The smallest baby ever brought into St. Christopher's was from Kwung Wah. He weighed three pounds. We had a lot of tiny babies coming in, so I'd made my own incubator for them. It was a small crib with heavy clear plastic on the sides, back and top. A single bulb hanging inside the transparent box kept the incubator at an even 80 degrees Fahrenheit.

One day a police officer brought a baby to us with bones sticking out everywhere. He was nothing but skin stretched thin over a tiny skeleton. The policeman said, "Honestly, I don't know why you bother with these ones. He probably won't last the night."

"Well," I told him, "I would rather have the baby die in comfort among caring, loving people, than die anonymously at Kwung Wah."

An abandoned baby brought to Muriel at St. Christopher's Baby Home. 1960.

Another one of the babies we took in from Kwung Wah weighed a mere four pounds, and stayed that way for a month. He just wouldn't or couldn't gain weight. The police came to take the baby away a month later, when he officially became a ward of the government, and I protested. Traveling outside the Home could have killed him. I politely informed the officers that I would continue to look after him until he was five or six pounds at least.

The next day I came into work and the baby was gone. I stood in the doorway, unable to speak. They had taken him away without any bottle, blanket, clean diapers or change of clothes. I roared into Kowloon city to the courthouse and demanded the baby be returned to me at once.

"It's the law, Tonge Tai," the judge said to me, gritting his teeth.

I clenched my fists together and said firmly, "With all due respect your Honour, I don't care about your law. I care about that baby. I care about his life. You're going to have to make some changes around here because we can't have these babies dying at the hands of the law, can we?" I shook my head and added, "You have to trust me anyway, your Honour. I could have sent you any one of our babies, and you wouldn't have known the difference. You also have to trust that I know what is best for them."

He looked at me and shook his head, grumbling something under his breath.

Shortly thereafter, an amendment was made to the law.

The Necessity of False Paperwork

I took it upon myself to write up fake abandonment papers for babies on a number of occasions. Sometimes it was the only thing I could do, with the well-being of the child in mind. In cases where the parents couldn't provide a decent life for their baby, or the baby couldn't get a passport or birth certificate in Hong Kong because they were born in China, I would ask them to leave the child on a chair in my office and go. They had six months in which to change their minds. I would call the police and tell them that a baby had been abandoned on our doorstep, parents unknown.

I didn't bend the rules for everyone though. A woman once abandoned her little girl in town, and the baby was quickly brought to us. A year later the mother returned with her two and a half year old son. Apparently she had tracked her daughter down, and had seen how well we looked after her. "You did such a great job with my daughter that I want you to take my little boy as well."

I told her that she needed to go and get adoption papers signed at the government office. The woman shook her head and said she couldn't look after him any more. "You have to take him," she pleaded.

"I will take him once you have signed the proper papers," I told her firmly. I didn't like the way she gripped her son's upper arm and yanked him about. Nor did I appreciate the way she presumed she could drop him off at St. Christopher's, like some unwanted puppy.

The woman bellowed that she would leave him out at the road if we didn't agree to take him immediately. I shrugged and stood firm. When she flew out of the room, I asked one of the staff members to follow her out the driveway and down to the road. Sure enough, the woman hopped onto a bus and left her toddler standing on the side of the road by himself. I called the police and reported that we had a "wandering child," which was different than a child who had been simply abandoned. While the wait for an abandoned child was six months to a year, a wanderer couldn't be put up for adoption until two years had passed, just in case the parents changed their minds. How could we let a child go back to a mother who was capable of getting on a bus and leaving him behind?

Well, at that time, a lovely English couple came in to adopt a child and they fell in love with the boy who had been left out at the road. Their eyes positively sparkled when they made him smile. I explained that the little boy had to stay with his younger sister because I didn't want them to be separated. The English couple didn't care. They agreed to take both children, even though they knew that if the biological mother turned up in the next two years, she had a right to take the little boy away from them. The kindly couple was willing to take the risk.

Luckily, this story ends happily. They are all still together, a healthy family. We never saw the biological mother again.

Peter

This story isn't so joyful, I'm afraid. One day, the Ministry of Children's Services sent a young mother to see us. She wanted to ask about temporary care for her three year old. When she rounded the corner of my office, I had to keep myself from staring at her grotesquely deformed face. Her cheeks and chin were covered in grossly enlarged pores and bubbled yellow skin, and her nose was bulbous and drooping. Some of my staff gathered around as she told us her story.

Apparently, she'd been the mistress of an American General for many years. He'd bought her a house, and everything she needed for a comfortable life in Hong Kong. One day she decided that she was going to get implants in her nose to make it a 'high nose', in an effort to look more western. Plastic surgery wasn't what it is today, and the doctor she saw filled the bridge of her nose with wax! I think she might have gotten some implants inserted into her cheeks and chin as well, because her entire face was disfigured. The procedure had obviously been sloppy, and the woman had ended up battling severe infections in her skin. Before long, her American boyfriend left her.

She got lonely, living in the large house all by herself. When she saw an advertisement in the newspaper for a dog for sale, she jumped at the chance for companionship. The people selling the dog told her that if she wanted him, she would have to take a baby as well. So, she paid 350 Hong Kong dollars, and got a dog, and a son all in one day. She named the boy Peter.

Now she had company, but her money was quickly running out. She was soon forced to sell the house, and most of her belongings. She took Peter to the government, and asked them for help. They sent her to St. Christopher's with the hopes that we might admit young Peter to our temporary care unit, which was a special service for people temporarily incapable of looking after their children. These were usually people with one or both parents in jail, or one parent on his or her deathbed.

I listened to her tearful story, and agreed to look after Peter for a while, even though I suspected that Peter hadn't been purchased at all. Just looking at him, with his pale skin, and wide eyes, it was easy to believe that he was part white. I suspected that she'd made up the story about the newspaper ad so that she could be exempted from responsibility. Actually, I couldn't even begin to guess what she was thinking. All I knew was that poor Peter needed a better home, with parents who really wanted him. I wanted to be able to put him up for adoption, and appealed to the government to write up the proper papers. I tried to reason with the officials, pointing out that purchasing a child was illegal, and therefore the mother wasn't legally bound to the boy.

As it turned out, the government also suspected that Peter was her flesh and blood, so they stood firm on their decision that he couldn't be put up for adoption.

After Peter had been in our care for one year (more than enough time for the St. Christopher's staff to fall in love with him), the mother with the disfigured face returned to take him away.

It was awful. Without so much as a thank-you, she grabbed him by the arm, and pulled him down the road. We never saw, or heard from them again.

Yee Chi Leung: The Boy with the Crooked Back

The Buddhist charity hospital, Kwong Wah, called me one afternoon wanting me to pick up five abandoned babies. I grabbed five small plastic tubs, and placed them in the back of our mission station wagon.

While waiting at the hospital's office for the papers to be prepared I decided to nose around the place, and peek into various treatment rooms. This was how I happened upon a large grey room filled with scrawny boys aged eight to sixteen. There were about fifteen of them in total, all with tuberculosis of the spine, their bodies severely hunched and misshapen. Some boys were seated along the perimeter of the room, while others shuffled back and forth aimlessly, not speaking or looking at anyone. All eyes were blank, mouths drawn downward. I was just about to throw the door open and burst into the room, just to see a spark of life, when the director of the hospital approached me from behind.

"Tell me about these boys, Dr. Yu," I whispered, keeping my eyes on the twisted shapes in the room.

He explained to me that the boys all had homes to go to, and were now waiting for the adoptive families to pick them up. "Well," he said, his voice hushing to a whisper, "all except Yee Chi Leung." Dr. Yu pointed to a little boy seated on the floor in the corner of the room. His dark head was bent over a book. The doctor sighed and explained that Yee Chi Leung had been left on their doorstep eight years ago, when he was two years old. I pressed my face closer to the window in the door.

The boy's head sunk into his neck, as if it was too heavy for his little body. His spine was crooked like a knotted tree branch, which made walking a laborious task. Apparently every Thursday, a teacher from the Red Cross came to tutor the boys in that room. She had reported to Dr. Yu that Yee Chi Leung was exceptionally brilliant for a ten year old.

At that moment Yee Chi Leung looked up from his book and turned his head toward me. I smiled at him and he warmly smiled back. His eyes were so soft and gentle, I instantly felt drawn to him.

"What if I take him back to St. Christopher's with me?" I suggested. "At least there he can play with other children and continue his studies."

Dr. Yu grinned and agreed. I walked into the room, crouched in front of Yee Chi Leung's and put my hand on his bony little shoulder. "Hello there, young man. My name is Mrs. Tonge. Everyone calls me Tonge Tai. How would you like to leave here with me today?"

I'll never forget the shine in Yee Chi Leung's eyes as we drove away. He sat on a box in the front seat so he could see out. The poor boy hadn't left the hospital in eight years! Everything outside the car window was a wonder to him, birds, flowers, trees, boats, other cars and people. His eyes were wide and shining as we drove.

Yee Chi Leung moved into one of the cottages with other boys his age. Like a worried mother I fretted over him for the first week or so. How would he get along with the other kids? Would the shock of change be too much for him?

After another week had passed I popped by his cottage to see how he was doing, and was horrified to hear peels of laughter rolling from the back yard. I shivered, and feared the worst. Yee Chi Leung was physically deformed, and children could be the cruelest creatures sometimes. With fists clenched I stormed around the corner, then halted, gaped in amazement at what I saw.

Yee Chi Leung was laughing the loudest, teetering up on a stool trying to hang his wet laundry on the line. The other boys stood below him, laughing with him as he made fun of his own disability. A couple of the boys stepped forward to help Yee Chi Leung keep his balance, while another boy reached up and pulled the laundry line closer to the ground.

I completely turned to liquid on the spot.

Later on that month, the orphan boys' housefather reported to me that Yee Chi Leung was one of the most pleasant boys in the cottage. He was always helpful and friendly. He was also the smartest student they had ever seen at the orphanage! As it turned out, he was able to complete three years of school in one year. Eventually we sent him to a church boarding school, thanks to North American Sunday School donations, where he became their champion chess player.

He went on to work in Kowloon as a secretary of an accounting firm. For someone with a crooked back, Yee Chi Leung knew how to stand tall. His kindness and inner strength inspired all who had the privilege of knowing him, myself included.

A Free Trip to Canada

When foreign couples were interested in adopting a Chinese baby, we were always hopeful that our orphans would have a new chance at a better life. About eighty percent of the adopted babies went to foreign homes, arranged by the International Social Services. The remaining twenty percent of babies usually went to local families or foreigners living in town. When meeting potential parents for our babies, I always erred on the side of caution. I was not in any position to give parents the benefit of the doubt. Often I refused to let couples take any of our babies.

For example, I once received three anonymous phone calls about a couple from the English Army who wanted to adopt. The caller said they were alcoholics. They didn't take a baby home with them, at least not from St. Christopher's.

Another English couple told me that they wanted to win the respect of their snooty neighbours by adopting a Chinese baby. They didn't get a baby from me.

One western woman, swathed in jewels, came in to see the orphans. When asked to hold one of the babies, she flatly refused, and instead had her servant carry the baby. Another American woman had a ridiculous concern. Looking down at a beautiful baby girl, the woman asked me, "How are we going to understand each other when she gets older? I don't speak Chinese!"

Good heavenly days! What nonsense.

Of course, clearing couples for adoption was a wonderful feeling. All we wanted was the best for our little ones.

On one occasion I was asked by the people at International Social Service to escort a group of five Chinese orphans to their new homes in the United States. This was a customary service back then. Today, couples adopting usually have to travel to the orphanage to pick up their baby when the time is right.

As a temporary employee of the airline, I received a complimentary ticket, and was allowed three weeks before I had to return. This meant a free trip home to see my family in Canada, whom I hadn't seen in over three years. I graciously accepted the offer. Walton and our amah, A Kwan, would stay behind to look after our four kids.

I was to escort three babies and two older boys, aged nine and ten. It sounded easy enough, but little did I know what I was getting myself into!

Chan Chat was a six-month-old girl whose mother had been hit by a bicyclist when she was pregnant. Bystanders rushed her to the hospital but didn't make it in time. She died upon arrival. The emergency doctor quickly performed a Caesarean section. The tiny baby was then brought to me at St. Christopher's, all adoption papers filled out and signed. The husband of the poor woman, Mr. Chan, had six other children and couldn't manage a seventh. We called her Chan Chut. Chan was her surname, and "Chut" means seven.

Tonge Bei Deuk, or Peter Tonge, was a bouncing eleven-month old boy, happy and healthy. He had come to us six months earlier, abandoned, tiny and fragile, with a disfigured hip. I didn't give him my last name out of conceit. The babies who came in with some kind of disability or disfigurement ended up with the name Tonge because very few Chinese people wanted their names to be taken by a child with imperfections. They considered it bad luck. So, those children got my family name instead.

The third baby was a healthy, ten month old girl, who was no trouble at all. Neither were the two older boys.

Luckily, I received generous assistance with the babies when we boarded the plane in Hong Kong and again in Japan where we had to wait in the transit lounge for our flight to Alaska. The trip had been smooth until we took off from Tokyo. We had been in the air for an hour when suddenly the pilot came on and announced that we had to return to Tokyo. "We have to dump some of our gas. Please prepare yourselves for an emergency landing."

I felt a jolt of adrenaline and clung to the briefcase that carried all of the children's paperwork. I remember feigning confidence for the sake of the two older boys, but inside I was praying, "Please, God, don't take me away from my family." I thought about how my mother must have prayed when her plane caught fire and began to plummet towards the ground.

I had the babies' seats padded with pillows. The airline didn't have any proper baby seats like you can get today. So the babies slept soundly in their comfortable bundles, despite the surrounding cries of their fellow passengers. My head between my knees, I muttered prayer after prayer, until I felt the familiar rumble of wheels making contact with tarmac. I sat up and exhaled, then looked outside my window at the flashing lights. Ambulances and fire trucks were racing alongside the airplane. Thankfully, we didn't need them. The landing had been fine, and we disembarked without incident.

Evidently the pilots had seen a flashing light on their console, telling them there was a fire on the plane. Turned out it was just a short, thank heavens.

It was well after midnight by this point, and we were all packed back into the transit lounge. I pushed some of the large comfortable chairs together to make a giant, padded playpen. It wasn't long before the three babies were asleep, curled up together. The two older boys dozed off on the floor beside the makeshift playpen.

Half an hour or so later we were ordered to clear out and get to a hotel. The next plane out would not be leaving until five the next morning. I didn't want to go anywhere. I'd finally gotten all the children to sleep! So I asked the airline representative in charge if we could stay put, motioning to the sleeping babies beside me. He gave in.

I had to be on guard the entire time, so I didn't sleep a wink. An elderly gentleman, who had also chosen to stay behind, approached me and asked if he could help. I appreciated the offer, and enjoyed his company for fifteen minutes or so, until he fell asleep, slumped in a chair beside the two boys on the floor.

The sweepers came by to clean up about an hour after the lounge had been cleared of most of the passengers. Clouds of dust filled the air, so I took some of the babies' clean diapers and covered their faces for protection. Next came the throngs of two-inch cockroaches, scuttling closer and closer to the children as the minutes passed. Just as my eyes started to droop, I had to snap awake and shoo the cockroaches away.

At 4 a.m. the waiting lounge once again came to life with passengers.

When the time came to board the plane, I was too tired to be nervous about any more emergency landings.

The orphans and I had three seats on either side of the plane. I sat on the aisle seat with two babies on my right. The other baby was across the aisle from me, where I could see her. The two boys kept their eyes on her as well.

We arrived in Alaska safe and sound at 9 p.m. I remember being perturbed when we landed in Alaska because the flight attendants exited the plane without so much as a look in my direction. I shouted after them, "Can somebody please help me carry these babies off the plane?"

One of the stewardesses hollered back at me that someone would be along shortly. Several minutes later I laughed when I saw two large workmen, oily and scruffy, walking down the narrow aisle towards us.

With warm smiles, they helped me wrap the babies in blankets, and carry them down to immigration.

When we stood in front of the immigration officer, he shrugged his shoulders and looked at me sheepishly. "I'm not sure what to do with you, ma'am," he said.

Apparently, a week prior to my departure from China, the law allowing orphans to enter the States had elapsed, and new legislation had yet to be written. My orphans had fallen into a procedural gap.

I was tired, stiff, and irritated. I asked him, "Sir, is this not the United States?"

"It is ma'am," he replied.

"Well then, my mandate was to bring these five children to their new homes in the United States. Here we are. My job here is done. They are all yours." With that, I turned on my heel and made for the door, leaving three babies and two young boys in front of the immigration desk. Two of the babies started crying. One crawled around on the ground, examining the lined pattern on the floor.

"Wait!" the man called after me, stepping out from behind the desk.

I turned and watched him approach. I explained with renewed patience that each child was going to a home, and if he had a problem with that, he could easily contact the waiting parents. He sighed and looked back at the crying babies.

"Fine. Go Ahead."

In Seattle, where I was to leave Chan Chut with her new family, we ran into more problems at the airport. The custom's officer noticed the basket of plastic flowers that my ten-year-old boy had brought with him as a gift for his new family. I hadn't thought anything of it because Hong Kong was famous for its plastic flowers. However, the custom's officer spotted a light film of yellow dust on the flowers and became suspicious.

He took the bouquet apart and found rare miniature plants growing at the bottom of the basket. "This is smuggling, lady," he growled at me. "We'll have to search through all your luggage."

I tried explaining that the boy hadn't known any better, but the man didn't believe me. He went about his task in a brutish, mechanical manner, searching the baby bags, and the rest of the two boys' luggage.

My suitcase was last. I found myself surrendering to the fact that I was probably about to be arrested. My bag was filled with precious gifts for my family: beautiful silks, undeclared jade jewelry, and electronic goods that were cheaper to buy in Hong Kong, such as cameras and tape recorders. All of it was undeclared. The officer opened the top section of my suitcase, which was filled with pamphlets for St. Christopher's Baby Home. I immediately plucked one off the top of the pile and pressed it into his hand.

"Please take this and read every word, sir," I said, giving his hand a squeeze. "Here, take more of them. Pass them on to your friends and relatives. The children are all orphans and are in need of funds to provide them with medical and educational supplies. We need all the help we can get. Any donation will do, any at all. Would you like to help us out today, sir?"

He grumbled something under his breath, stuffed the pamphlet into his back pocket, then shut the suitcase and handed it back to me.

I thanked him, and bustled out of there as quickly as I could. We handed Chan Chut over to her gushing parents, said goodbye, and continued on our way. We had a tight schedule to keep.

Our next flight was to Indianapolis. By this time, our sleeping patterns were completely disrupted, and the two older boys had fallen ill. I tried in vain to get the babies to sleep, while tending to the vomiting older boys. Being sick and nervous is a vile combination. I had to resort to giving sleeping pills to the babies, much to the delight of the ornery passengers around us who had been trying unsuccessfully to get some sleep themselves.

At 5 a.m. we finally landed in Indianapolis, where I managed to get the two babies, two boys and their bags to the waiting area by myself. I was expecting one of the adoption agency representatives to meet us, but there was no one in sight. The children and I got as comfortable as we could, and waited. Three hours passed before I heard the clicking of high heels approaching us. A young flight attendant leaned over me and asked, "Are you Mrs. Tonge?"

Groggily I nodded.

"I've come to take Peter to Chicago. His new family is waiting for him there."

I had her wait with the other children while I took Peter into the washroom to clean and change him.

The flight attendant signed the necessary paperwork, and took Peter into her arms and off they went.

Next stop, New York, where the remaining three children were meeting their families. Upon our arrival, one of the flight attendants asked me to keep the children seated until the rest of the passengers had disembarked. I was delighted to see a crowd of thirty people or so, families and friends holding signs, balloons and teddy bears. Despite the warm reception, the two boys clung to me, burying their faces in my skirt. The baby whimpered in my arms.

I advised the adoptive parents to hold off on the celebrations for a little while, as it was important to let the children adjust to their new surroundings. They needed a quiet transition. Tearfully, I said goodbye to the brave little souls who were about to begin promising new lives.

Next, I flew on to Buffalo where my family from Niagara Falls, Ontario was to pick me up that night. By the time I left the airport at 6 p.m., I knew I had to make a change of plans. I checked myself into a hotel room, and felt my limbs turn to pudding on the soft bedding.

"Gwen," I said to my sister over the phone, "better not come until tomorrow morning. I can't move at the moment."

Dad, Lydia, and Gwen came to fetch me the next morning. It was the first time I'd seen them since we'd left Canada for Hong Kong, four years earlier!

As we were crossing the border into Canada, the burly border man leaned out his window and asked where we were born. We answered him in unison:

"England," said my father.

"Norway," said Lydia.

"China," said Gwen and I.

All of us began to laugh, including the border man (which was a rare sight indeed!). "Let's start over again," he said, smiling. Each of us spoke in turn, answering his questions. By this time I was so tired with officials and with questions and borders and delays that when he asked me, "Have you anything to declare?" I said:

"Yes. I have a whole suitcase of goods from Hong Kong. Wonderful things like jade, cameras, silk scarves. They are all gifts for my family. I've been travelling for a week now. I came from Hong Kong. I volunteer at an orphanage there, and was asked to escort three babies and two children to their adoptive families in the U.S. We had a crash landing in Japan. Then had stopovers in Alaska, Indianapolis and New York. I've had about five hours of sleep in the past seven days, but now my family has come down from Canada to get me, and save me from having to step on one more airplane for a little while. I have two more weeks before I have to go back to Hong Kong. Would you like a pamphlet with information on our Baby Home in Hong Kong? We are always looking for donations from kind souls like you. Every little bit helps, sir."

He looked me long and hard in the face, and cleared his throat. "Thank you ma'am," he said, "that will be all."

We were on our way. After he waved us through the border, and we were driving on Canadian soil, I felt my shoulders finally relax.

A Risky Visit

Security along the Hong Kong border was very tight in the days of the Communist Revolution. No unauthorized person was allowed within two miles of the border to China. Communist soldiers paced back and forth along border crossings, trying to prevent Chinese people from escaping to Hong Kong. Hundreds of thousands of educated people sought refuge in the British colony because in China they were at risk of being killed by the Red Guard.

(Mao convinced youth to band together and cleanse the country of people who thought they were better than average because they had educations. Suddenly students were killing their teachers, doctors, engineers, and anyone who had connections with the West. The Red Guard destroyed all foreign music, books, and art they could get their hands on. It was Mao Tse-tung's way of restoring his all-powerful status, which had begun to dwindle during the first years of Communist rule. By convincing China's youth that something foul was afoot, and that educated people couldn't be trusted, he managed to create a rebellion so powerful that it crippled the country for nearly a decade.)

Right around Christmas time, St. Christopher's Baby Home received dozens of infant layettes, or little sleepers as they might be called. We didn't need many at that time, so we came up with the idea to give a layette to every baby born at Christmas in the clinics around the New Territories.

In all there were ten clinics, including one in Sha Tau Kok, which was a town that straddled the border between China and Hong Kong. The only people allowed back and forth over the border were the residents, who had to carry identification at all times. After the town was divided, people lived on the Hong Kong side but worked in the China side of Sha Tau Kok, and vice versa. The circumstances were complicated.

Getting to the clinic in this border city should have been impossible, but I had connections. My friend Dr. Perry knew the doctor at Sha Tau Kok, so he made all the arrangements, and then even offered to drive me there. We passed right through the guarded gates outside the city and made our way to the clinic, where a luncheon awaited us.

Before we had to leave, I asked the doctor if I could take a quick walk around the town. I'd never been to Sha Tau Kok, and wanted to explore a little bit. He told me that I could walk around, as long as I didn't have a camera or anything in my hands. Because of the influx of Chinese refugees sneaking into Hong Kong, the Communist soldiers were patrolling all the time. If I wandered around taking pictures of the mountains, or the buildings, it might look like I was going to sneak information to friends in China.

I walked through the town, then right up to the border, with China on the opposite side of the barbed-wire fence. I walked along the fence, out onto a pier that was divided in half by the border. As I strolled towards the water, three Communist soldiers—guns in hand—walked on the other side of the fence. I stood at the end of the pier, admiring the water and mountains, studying the colours and shapes for a future painting. I tried my best not to look troublesome but those soldiers mirrored my every move, step by step, except I was smiling and they were not. They were like grey shadows. My bright yellow sweater against their drab grey uniforms stuck out like banana on a boot rack.

I returned to the clinic in time to meet up with Dr. Perry, who then drove me back to Chung Chi. My doctor friends had stuck their necks out far for me this time. Not many people could say they'd been inside the city of Sha Ta Kok.

Three days later, Walton and I were invited to our neighbours' house for dessert and coffee. A British officer friend of theirs was visiting, and after brief introductions, we learned that he was the head of security at the Hong Kong border. I opened my big mouth and said, "Oh! I was just in your area a few days ago. Sha Ta Kok! It's such a beautiful...."

His mouth swung open and he narrowed his eyes. It suddenly dawned on me that I was potentially blowing the cover of my doctor friends who had managed to sneak me through the gates.

"How did you do that? How did you get inside Sha Tau Kok? Even the Governor General isn't allowed to go there!" the head of security said.

I cleared my throat and stood up, saying something ridiculous about having to leave to visit some sick people across town. In a haze of apologies, and with everyone including Walton staring at me, I left. I didn't want to risk getting my doctor friends into trouble by letting anything else slip.

I made no more risky visits to border towns after that. Obviously I wasn't cut out for sneaking around or knowing when to keep my mouth shut.

Chinese Medicine

At the end of the day, when I left St. Christopher's, I had my own family to take care of, and we always had something going on in our flat.

One of the exciting things about working as a health care professional in China was seeing first hand the secrets of ancient Chinese medicine. Some western doctors might look down their noses at the old ways, but I still found it fascinating.

Once, our second son David twisted his ankle while playing with friends. I had a good look at the ankle and determined that, although it was swollen and bruised, it was not broken. Our dear amah, A Kwan, had a look and went about concocting her own remedy. (I should explain that in Cantonese, placing an "a," pronounced Ah, in front of someone's name is a sign of affection and respect.)

While A Kwan busied herself by boiling six eggs to put on David's ankle, Walton asked me impatiently, "Why are you letting A Kwan waste six eggs like this? You know whatever she's going to do with them won't do any good for his ankle."

"It is already doing a lot of good," I said. "A Kwan feels good because she is taking care of David, and David feels good because he is being taken care of. Why worry about a few eggs?"

After placing the eggs on David's ankle, A Kwan had second thoughts, and decided that she was going to fetch A So, who was the caretaker of the Chung Chi College library. He was also the local expert in Chinese massage, and was respected for his knowledge throughout the medical community. He was a thin wisp of a man in his sixties without a speck of skin that wasn't deeply creased.

I'd met him several months before when I had been called into the library one afternoon. His nose had been bleeding for several hours, and he was getting worried. Gingerly I removed the coarse plant leaves he'd used to plug his bloody nostrils. Once his nose was cleared it took no time at all to stop the bleeding. A So had been amazed. So when A Kwan summoned him to go to our house to have a look at David's ankle he was more than happy to oblige.

He shuffled into our home and sat down to give the swollen ankle a thorough examination. He came to the conclusion that it wasn't broken. Walton, A Kwan, David and I watched as A So rubbed his hands together rapidly and then vibrated his fingers along the nerve pathways and pressure points in David's ankle and lower leg. David fell fast asleep while his ankle magically twitched in all directions. A So applied a thick, brown, foul-smelling paste to the whole foot.

Walton pulled me aside and whispered, "Why are you letting him do all that voodoo nonsense? We don't know what's in that brown stuff. It's stinking up the whole flat!"

"Settle down," I said calmly. "The smell is a small price to pay."

"But what about—"

"Chinese medicine won't harm him in any way, Walton," I said, patting him on the shoulder. ' Don't be such a fuddy-duddy."

A So dropped in to see David every day for a week, after which David was able to walk normally again.

Miraculous Baby Booties

During the chilly winter months in Hong Kong, I would appeal to church organizations for baby booties, among other things. After receiving bags upon bags of booties, Leslie and I would take them into the marketplaces. Young mothers walked around with their babies snug in what was called a *bo ma*, or cloth horse, a padded backpack-type of thing. The babies were covered in a cape and hood, but their little bare feet usually stuck out the sides of the cloth horse, exposed to the chilly gusts. Leslie and I walked around sliding warm pairs of hand-knit booties onto their feet, much to the surprise and delight of the mothers.

A Canadian therapist from a ward in British Columbia wrote me one winter to say that a group of her patients had knit a large pile of booties for us. Learning how to knit had been a therapeutic project for them. Upon receiving bags upon bags of booties, I was disappointed to discover that none of them could be worn. They were red, blue, pink, purple ... so many beautiful, bright colours! But the sizes were all off. They were too big, too small, or too misshapen, so that no baby foot could fit inside them. Some had ankles that were so narrow I could barely slide my finger inside.

Just before the bags of malformed booties had arrived, a neighbour's amah had been asking me if I had any spare wool or yarn. She wanted to make an adult-sized sweater. I didn't have any wool at the time so I hadn't inquired any further into her project. After going through the booties from the psychiatric ward, and determining that none of the booties was wearable, I presented them to the amah. She told me that she was going to make a sweater from the bootie wool and send it to a Communist cadre in China. At the receipt of the sweater he would give the amah's elderly parents enough food for a month.

"Are you absolutely sure your parents will get the food he is promising?" I asked.

"Yes. I have made trades like this with him before. My parents have reported that he does give them food. Without his help they would be starving."

She took the box of booties and went to work unraveling. After a month she showed me her masterpiece. It was the most colourful, striped sweater I had ever seen. "What do you think?" she asked, beaming.

From booties, to a sweater, to a month's supply of food!

"It's stunning," I said.

Walton, the kids, and I returned to Canada on furlough in 1962 after we'd been living in Hong Kong for five wonderful years. In the days since my childhood the church had changed the furlough rotation from every seven years to every five years.

By that time St. Christopher's truly needed a supervisor for the Baby Home who could live on-site, and that wasn't me. I'd given them all that I could by that point.

When I think about the many opportunities my life has offered up, my incredible experiences at St. Christopher's Baby Home are high on the list. I went from being a young, timid, mother of four, to an iron-willed mother of hundreds. I had learned to fight for what I believed in. Without a doubt St. Christopher's was where I grew into myself.

Chapter 10

Grandma's Umbrella

June 2006

At the beginning of June in Yangshuo it rained for two weeks straight. Most umbrellas there, unfortunately, were not made to last. All around me people grumbled about umbrellas falling apart, leaking, or ripping. My fellow English teachers went through as many as three umbrellas in just two months. I was grateful for the sturdy umbrella that Grandma had sent with me when I left Canada. "You will need a good umbrella," she had said.

I was on my way to pick up some fruit at the market, and had my strong, Canadian umbrella in hand. The rain was just beginning to let up. While crossing the street, I saw a petite, elderly man walking steps in front of me with the shabbiest umbrella I'd ever seen.

Peasants in Yangshuo were as ubiquitous as tourists. Probably more so. Like the tourists, those of us who were more permanently settled in the small town tended to see past them after a while. They become a part of the scenery, like bamboo, or noodle vendors. I knew I was human, but I never wanted to become desensitized to the world around me.

I walked faster until I hovered over the little man with the umbrella, and could look down and inspect the patches in his umbrella's material. (I'd gotten used to being a giantess compared to most people in Yangshuo, especially the older folks with their stooped posture.) The stitches around his faded patches had pulled apart in some places, and were non-existent in others. Where there were no patches, the umbrella fabric was stretching and straining, and new holes were beginning to form. I could see right through one hole to the man's round, grey head.

His thin, wrinkled hand gripped the umbrella tight, despite the fact that rain was dampening the hair at the back of his neck.

I stopped to feel and smell some ripe mangos at my favourite stand. My friendly fruit-seller friend waited with her plastic bag ready, watching as I put the mango back down and stepped back out onto the wet street. I looked for the shabby umbrella, but the man had disappeared. Colourful umbrellas were everywhere, weaving back and forth on the street as people avoided puddles. I scanned the sides of the street where people were picking through produce spread on the ground. I spotted the elderly man, his umbrella held to one side, as he tossed one cob aside and slowly bent to examine another.

"*Zhe ge bu hao*," I said, pointing to his shoddy umbrella.

He turned to look at me, confused. I said again, "*Zhe ge bu hao. Wo xiang gei ni wo de.*" (This is no good. I want to give you mine.) I realized when the man continued to stare at me blankly that he might only speak the local language, as was the case with many farmers from the countryside. I placed my colourful, rip-resistant umbrella in his hand. He glanced down at the gift, and then looked beside me as someone translated my Mandarin into the local language. He glimpsed at his umbrella, sitting upside-down on the dirty pavement, and then held my umbrella up over his head. I turned and smiled to the friendly translator, who nodded politely back to me.

To avoid the man feeling awkward about my public offering, and obliged to give me something in return, I quickly stepped back into the street. Without looking back, I strolled up the fruit market street, on the way to buying myself a new umbrella. My throat tightened as I thought about Grandma's umbrella on its way to a new home. It had been such a simple encounter, but I couldn't wait to tell her the story.

Chapter 11

From Babies to Opium Addicts

Hong Kong 1963-1968

We spent our 1962 furlough in London, Ontario, where both Walton and I travelled around to neighbouring cities and towns, giving talks about the work of the church in China. Our kids went to school, and then to the cottage on Lake Chandos in the summer. When September rolled around it and was time for us to fly back to our lives and work in Hong Kong. The five of us returned to Chung Chi College, where Walton continued his work as Chaplain, and Murray (fourteen), David (twelve) and Elizabeth (six) went back to the British School.

Leslie had stayed back in Canada to finish her final year of high school, and to prepare for university. As difficult as it was to leave her behind with Walton's sister, we knew the importance of Leslie's education. Leaving loved ones behind was an accepted part of missionary life back then. It was accepted that by sixteen you were old enough to live apart from your family.

Apart from Leslie's absence, our lives on Chung Chi campus picked up just as it had been before we left on furlough. Until we met Ho Ying, that is.

As a part of my contributions to the campus community at Chung Chi, I would pay visits to several of the neighbouring families, and offer whatever assistance I could, if any was needed. The Chen family was particularly troubled. The father was a drunk, and would frequently beat his wife and three young daughters. I visited them often to offer what help and support I could.

One afternoon, during one of my visits to the Chen girls, I met their young neighbour, Ho Ying. She was a shy, skinny little thing, eight or nine years old. Out of the corner of my eye, I saw her peering carefully around the corner of the house, watching me as I talked with Mrs. Chen. I learned that Ho Ying was the daughter of one of the property staff on campus, who worked long hours and was very rarely home. Poor little Ho Ying didn't have anyone to play with because most of the children her age were too busy with piano lessons or after-school pursuits. Ho Ying's father didn't have much money, so he had no choice but to send her to a low-end school. Our amah, A Kwan, informed us that little Ho Ying was very bright, but malnourished.

Being a kind and giving soul, A Kwan asked if we could possibly let her live with us for a little while. A Kwan's husband had died when they were young, and she'd never re-married or had any children of her own, so she took a special interest in Ho Ying. Walton and I discussed it and agreed to take her into our home.

Ho Ying's father had worked for the Nationalist party and like so many others had been forced to leave China. Ho Ying's mother and brother lived with him in Hong Kong for a short time, but her mother wasn't happy, and soon returned to China. She was pregnant with Ho Ying. One day, when Ho Ying was six, her mother was standing out on the balcony hanging red decorations for Chinese New Year when she slipped and fell to her death. A short time later, Ho Ying's father had her and her brother brought to Hong Kong to live with him in his small apartment on Chung Chi campus.

At first, the poor girl was too frightened to even set foot in our house. She had never spoken with foreigners before, and trembled whenever I tried to invite her inside. She was comfortable with A Kwan, so they lived together in A Kwan's room for the first little while. Any time I wanted to ask Ho Ying a question I had to speak to her through A Kwan. In Cantonese, with Ho Ying right there in the room, I would say to A Kwan, "I am going to be cutting Elizabeth's hair this afternoon. Could you please ask Ho Ying if she would like hers cut as well?" A Kwan would pass on my message, and then Ho Ying would give me her reply through A Kwan. That's how shy she was.

Ho Ying eventually adjusted to her loud foreign friends, and learned to fit in with my children. She and Elizabeth became playmates, and slowly little Ho Ying let herself become a part of our family, even eating meals with us.

With the help of church funds, we sent Ho Ying to a prestigious Hong Kong school for bright students. When it came time for our family to return to Canada, I wanted to take Ho Ying with us but her father declined the offer. She was his daughter, and Hong Kong was Ho Ying's home.

After our family had left Hong Kong, Ho Ying went off to university where she earned her Bachelor's degree, followed by a Master's degree in business. She is now a successful manager of a large battery-making company in Hong Kong and has made quite a name for herself in the business sector. Even after we left, Ho Ying remained close with my family. She is my Chinese daughter, after all. In the few times we have since visited Hong Kong, Ho Ying and her husband Daniel have taken extremely good care of us!

Ho Ying in Hong Kong. 1967

A Child Care Centre in the Sunken City

While living in Hong Kong the second time around I didn't spend as much time at St. Christopher's. Wanting to stretch my wings a little bit and try something new, I wasted no time in finding other places to offer my services.

One such place was the Child Care Centre in what was then known as the "Sunken City," or "Walled City," in the region of Hong

Kong known as Kowloon. It was called sunken because you had to walk down a set of stairs to get to it, and walled because of the ten-foot high wall that had at one time protected the city from the rest of Hong Kong. It was also sometimes called the "Forbidden City" because it was dangerous, and had been abandoned years ago by both the Chinese and Hong Kong authorities. It was an urban island, ~~ten square miles~~, surrounded by Hong Kong, but overseen by no one. *6 acres*

Naturally, the Sunken City became a haven for drug dealers, addicts and criminals hiding from the law. Some folks who lived there had jobs in Hong Kong, but most squatted in small rooms or shacks and stole money for opium.

The streets throughout the Sunken City were about six feet wide, and usually had some sort of open sewage system flowing down the middle in foul, brown streams. Dead rats, cats, and bags of garbage gathered on either side of its streets in stinky, messy clumps. Hardly any sunlight filtered to street level because the buildings rose up for several stories, leaving only a tiny sliver of sky exposed. Children had nowhere to play. There were no schools, or parks. Residents didn't even have their own water supply; they had to illegally tap into the Hong Kong water main. Corpses were often tossed onto the Hong Kong streets in the middle of the night, left for city officials to deal with. There were no cemeteries or crematoriums in the Sunken City.

A British nurse named Katherine had been called into this area to tend to a sick child, and had been disgusted by what she found when she stepped down the stairs into the city streets. Sick children slumped in dirty corners everywhere she looked, with their parents away or high on opium. She saw drug addicts lying face down in their own vomit. Katherine managed to find the sick child's home, but had to wander through cramped streets and dripping alleyways to get there. She realized that the children living in the filthy city didn't have any schools or medical care available to them, and decided then and there that she would see what she could do. That was how the Child Care Centre came to be. Katherine eventually asked me to work as one of the nurses, and I accepted on the spot.

A street in the Sunken City. 1967.

Muriel helping people in the line up inside the Childcare Clinic, 1965

The Banquet

Every morning, children from all over the Sunken City gathered outside our door to wait for a serving of milk and nutritious biscuits, kindly donated by church charities. Finally mothers and children had a place to turn to.

We saw all types of ailments at the Child Care Centre. Our small waiting area, with wooden benches along the walls, was always packed with patients. Usually there weren't enough seats. People stood pressed together, shoulder to shoulder, like barnyard animals at the trough. I remember one day seeing a child with measles sitting next to another child sick with strep throat.

One day a mother arrived with a toddler who had fallen into a pot of boiling gruel. The child's arm was covered in slimy third-degree burns, from hand to elbow. It was common in the Sunken city for families of eight, nine, or ten to be crammed into one tiny room. They cooked most of their meals on the floor, over small charcoal braziers, and this poor child had stumbled over to the pot and fallen in while her mother's back was turned. Unfortunately the family had waited three days before they'd brought the little girl to see us, by which time the burns had become badly infected. The dead skin had turned black, and her hand had gone completely numb. It took a lot of work to get the burns cleared up, but thankfully we were able to save the youngster's arm.

On another occasion a man arrived with an abscess the size of a ping-pong ball bulging behind his ear. I sat him down, and had just lanced the abscess to let it drain, when six representatives from Project Concern, an American charity organization, walked in to the clinic. Project Concern had provided us with all of our medical kits and tools. A silver-haired gentleman from the charity stood right behind me, keenly observing the fellow with the abscess.

"Hello," I said. It was nice to talk to a healthy visitor.

"Hello."

"Where are you from?"

"The United States."

"Mm-hmm, and what do you do there?" I said, dabbing at the abscess with a cotton swab. Despite my confidence in the operation, my cheeks began to flush under the man's unbroken gaze, as if I was back at nurses' training, undergoing an assessment.

He casually told me he was the Chief of Surgery at some big hospital in the States. I froze, holding my cotton swab in mid-air. I quickly composed myself, turned to face the man and said, "Well, the wash basin is in the corner over there, sir. Soap and water are on the counter. Would you be so kind as to take over for me? I could use a break."

"Gladly."

He washed up in the water bin and looked around at our counter top, cluttered with jars and medical supplies. He picked up one of the scalpels and inspected it closely, then proceeded to give me a mini-lecture on lancing and draining abscesses as he continued where I'd left off.

Although it was a child-care clinic, we treated adults as well as children for the simple reason that it was impossible for us to turn anyone away. Sometimes we were required to go out and visit the seriously ill in their homes. On one such occasion, I was called out to see a young woman deep in the heart of the Sunken City who was in critical condition. I ventured into the narrow streets and asked some men hunched over their opium pipes for directions. An elderly drug addict led me into a squalid flat. Eleven or twelve men around the perimeter of the front room lay prostrate on straw mats smoking opium. They lifted their heads enough for their foggy eyes to follow me as I bustled past, a blur of white.

I found my patient at the back of a windowless room, stretched out on the floorboards. She had given birth two months ago, and had since developed a breast abscess the size of a tennis ball. It was bright red and very tender. Her temperature was spiking, and her pulse raced like a small bird's. If left untreated the infection would start to poison her body through her bloodstream and would eventually kill her.

I had unwittingly stumbled into a delicate situation. If I treated the woman and she died, I knew the opium addicts would become angry. Possibly even violent. On the other hand, if I didn't treat her and she died, again I'd be in trouble. The bottom line: I wanted her to live. I had to treat her, regardless of the risks.

I took a deep breath and carefully cut into the bulbous abscess. Yellowish-green fluid trickled down the side of her breast. After doing a quick scratch test to make sure she wasn't allergic to penicillin, I administered the drug to fight infection, and then cleaned up the small incision on her breast. She rolled her head to one side and looked at me after swallowing the penicillin. I instructed her to get lots of rest.

After that first operation I visited her every day for a week to change her dressings and check on her progress. After seven days she was sitting up and chatting with me. By that time I was walking into the flat to smiles and even a couple of waves from the opium addicts.

"Morning Tonge Tai."

"Morning fellas."

Towards the centre of the Sunken City was a small open square—about twenty by twenty feet—where heroin addicts gathered every morning at eleven to wait for the delivery of their drugs. Once they picked up their stash, they retreated to their smelly alleyways where they took a small square of tin, bent it in half, and placed a drop of gooey heroin in the crease. They would hold a small flame from an oil lamp underneath the tin until the heroin bubbled and smoked. The tiny waft of smoke gave the addicts their high. They called this process "chasing the dragon."

I had been told not to worry about the crowds of addicts. As long as they got their supply, and as long as you didn't carry a purse with you, they were harmless. One day a request came to the clinic for a nurse to visit a sick child who lived on the other side of the infamous square. "Don't be nervous," one of my co-workers said to me. "Just be friendly, and everything will be fine."

As I stepped around the squatting men, I smiled and commented cheerfully on the beautiful weather. "How are you doing today?" I asked one older gentleman who was scowling at my white uniform.

"Not good," he grunted. "We can't get it today."

I stopped walking and noticed how the crowd of addicts were skulking closer to me, moaning and shuffling like Halloween monsters. A prickly shiver of ice ran down my back. I swallowed and began to inch backwards, taking care not to trip over anyone behind me. When I reached the safety of the street, I turned and ran all the way back to the Child Care Centre.

By the time I caught my breath I felt somewhat foolish. Good heavens, a sick child needed medical care, and I let a few sluggish drug addicts scare me away!

I marched back to the square, fists tight. Thankfully by that time the crowd had dispersed somewhat. There were no grumpy addicts in sight, and I found my way to the sick child with no trouble at all.

The atmosphere in the Sunken City grew very tense during the Cultural Revolution. Because it was a part of China, the people of the Sunken City disliked the West. They avoided westerners in the streets, and turned their backs on us as we walked past. Before the Cultural Revolution I used to walk into stores and homes to chat with people. All of a sudden no one wanted to talk to me any more. I knew it wasn't personal, but it still stung a little bit. I did my best to keep quiet, and lower my head so as to not embarrass anyone by making eye contact. It was really the only thing I could do in those difficult and confusing times. Thankfully, mothers and their children still flocked to the school and Child Care Centre seeking education and medical aid. They couldn't afford to let politics get in the way.

Eventually the Hong Kong government assumed control of the Sunken City. Buildings were burned down and never rebuilt. In 1987, with the agreement of Chinese and Hong Kong authorities, it was decided to clear the area of inhabitants and turn the city into an enormous park in the heart of Kowloon, which is what it is today. Over time, the 60 000 residents of the Sunken City became assimilated into Hong Kong. As the economy improved, I can only hope that they were able to find jobs as the economy improved, and live more comfortably.

What If He Wets?

I had just spent the day shopping, and my legs felt like wood. My joints ached, and my feet were throbbing. The air was hot and as heavy as steam. When I got on the city bus to go back to Chung Chi, I sank gratefully into the last remaining seat, right behind the bus driver.

A few stops later, a young woman got on with a baby on her back, a baby in one arm, a toddler beside her, and two chickens under the other arm. Delicate lines of sweat trickled down her temples and chest. She stood beside me and held onto the back of my seat.

"Can I hold your baby for you?" I offered. She gratefully plopped her fat one-year-old onto my lap. He smiled up at me as I curled my arm around him. He was naked except for the stained and sweaty undershirt that stretched over his belly.

Moments later an officer stepped onto the bus. After taking one look at me, the only foreigner on the bus, he asked the bus driver in a booming voice, "What do you think she'll do if the baby wets on her lap?"

The bus driver sniggered, glancing back at me. The baby bounced happily on my leg. I felt the dozens of eyes on me, watching to see what I would do. What if the baby did pee on my lap? Would I throw a fit and thrust him back to the mother?

"Well," I said loudly in Cantonese, "I have had babies wet my lap many times. One more won't hurt."

I looked up at the bus driver and caught him smiling at me.

By the time we arrived at my stop the crowd had pushed the mother and her children and chickens to the back of the bus. I instructed the people in the seat behind me to hand the baby back to her. The half-naked little boy bounced from person to person, like a fat, smiling ball, until he was back in the crook of his mother's arm.

Chapter 12

Leaving Again for the Last Time

1967

 A year before we were to leave China for Canada for another furlough in 1968, Walton and I realized we would have no extra money for travelling. The church board had given us only enough money for basic travel expenses. Walton and I hoped to take our kids to visit our relatives in Porthleven, England, as my father had once done with my sisters and me. We needed money to turn our trip to Canada into more of an adventure. As much as I loved my volunteer work at the Child Care Centre, I needed a paying job. And so the hunt began.

 My dear friend Dr. Perry would go up in a helicopter once a month to tend to families in isolated mountain villages. I had pestered him in the past to take me with him sometime, so that I could go for a helicopter ride and take pictures. He'd told me, "Tonge Tai, I'd love to take you but you aren't insured for this. I can't risk it."

 "How about this, Ron: If we do not crash, then insurance isn't a problem. If we do crash, and are killed, then you and I won't be here to worry about it. What do you think?"

 Not long after that conversation he took me along in the helicopter with him, as his nurse.

 It didn't exactly work out as well as I'd hoped. The children in the remote mountain villages hid behind their mothers and cried when they saw me, a ghostly foreigner. (Ron, being Portuguese-Chinese, wasn't as frightfully odd-looking as I was.)

 Months later, I asked Ron if he would consider hiring me as his clinic's head nurse. "Absolutely not," was his response.

 "Why on earth not?"

"Because I want you always as a friend. And because you would turn the whole place upside down."

"Yes," I replied, "And I would start with your obstetric clinic. It is stuck in the dark ages, Ron."

He didn't give me the job.

A clinic had just opened in Sha Tin, a town two miles away from Chung Chi College. They were short on nursing staff, so I went to see the principal matron for Hong Kong clinics and Hospitals.

She said stiffly, "We don't hire ex-patriots here."

"What do you mean?" I asked.

"We don't hire anyone who wasn't born in China, Hong Kong, or Taiwan."

"Well," I said, "I was born in China."

"That may very well be, but England doesn't recognize Canadian doctors or nurses, so naturally Hong Kong doesn't recognize or accept them either."

"If you look in your files you will see that Saskatchewan, one of the Canadian provinces, recognizes England's medical community and visa versa. I happen to be a graduate from the University of Saskatchewan."

The woman huffed. "Well, we need nurses trained in midwifery."

"Not only do I have training in midwifery, but I have additional training in treatment of tuberculosis. I do believe it is one of your worst killers here, am I right?"

"We need people who speak the language."

"I am fluent in both Mandarin and Cantonese."

The woman shook her head, and told me that there were no jobs available. Disgruntled, I left the office.

A short time later I heard that the Canadian Trade Commissioners office wanted a nurse for eleven months in the immigration office. The opportunity and timing were perfect. I phoned the Canadian doctor and he said he had heard of me, and that I had been highly recommended. He wanted to have me in for an interview.

I knew, however, that somewhere in their file system there were reports on Mr. and Mrs. Tonge, and how over the years we had been loudly critical of the immigration policies of Hong Kong. We were never reprimanded for expressing our views, but I doubted this man was likely to think highly of either my husband or me. Still, it was worth a try.

I sat down across from the doctor and smiled at him. His hard eyes looked me up and down and said, "You're Mrs. Tonge?"

"Yes."

"I thought when I spoke to you on the phone that you were Chinese."

"No sir, as you can see, I'm not Chinese. Is that a problem?"

He scratched his head. "I thought you were either Chinese, or married to a Chinese man."

"Well," I said, "how do you know that I'm not married to a Chinese man?"

He looked up from his papers. "Are you?"

I couldn't lie. His mind was already made up. I didn't get that job either.

Before I knew it the time for furlough was upon us. I never did find that paying job, but I was able to sell some of my paintings to friends in our community. I didn't make much, but it was better than nothing.

Had Walton and I known that we weren't ever going to live in Hong Kong again, we could have sold some of our belongings for extra money. As it was, we left our apartment completely set up for our return. We thought we'd only be gone a year.

When we returned to Canada, however, Walton came down with sarcoidosis, which is a cousin of tuberculosis. He had also developed a kidney stone as a result of the disease. He lost a great deal of weight, and became easily tired. His doctors recommended that his health be closely monitored. Three of our four children were in university by that time so it just didn't feel right to return to China and divide our family in two again. The decision was made to stay in Toronto.

I have returned to China and Hong Kong several times since those days, but only for brief visits to see how my orphans have been doing, and to visit old friends. My children and I travelled to Hong Kong together in the fall of 2004, and had a wonderful time visiting all our favourite spots, and marveling over how much the city had changed. It was all so long ago, but when I look at pictures, or tell some of the stories ... goodness, it seems like yesterday.

*

Chapter 13

The Beginning

February 2006

Hong Kong was steamy and polluted. My eyes took a moment to adjust to the sunlight as I stepped out of the airport arrivals lounge. The shock of temperature difference, exiting the frosty air-conditioned airport and entering the heat, left me feeling feverish.

Ho Ying was smaller than I imagined her to be. She was petite, stylish, and serious. Her face was smooth and calm, but her sparkling eyes betrayed her energy. She bustled me along, with one hand on my luggage cart, leading me towards her car. More air-conditioning. She was talkative as she drove, excited that I had finally arrived. She had heard much about me from my parents and grandma, and had been planning to take me on a whirlwind tour of Hong Kong before I left for Yangshuo.

After unpacking and getting acquainted with my hostess it was almost time for dinner, and I was fighting the onslaught of fatigue. It had been a long, taxing journey from Toronto, and it was catching up with me. However, Ho Ying had another idea. She wanted to take me to see the school my mom, uncles and aunt attended. Though my eyes were barely slits, and my feet were swollen and aching, I let myself be whisked out of the apartment into the steamy heat. I was in Hong Kong, after all, and I was full of traveller's adrenaline, a most potent and practical juice.

I had many places on my list of hotspots in Hong Kong, none of which were featured in the *Lonely Planet* traveller's guide. It took four days, but I managed to see the school that played a huge part of my mom's life while she lived there. I visited Chung Chi campus, where the Tonges lived for ten years, including the pathway where my mom and uncles used to cut through the woods to catch their train to school. I stopped off to visit the family's flat, the clinic where Grandma worked, and the church where Granddad preached.

The Banquet

Emily and Man-On, one of Muriel's St. Christopher's babies, standing outside Walton Tonge's church on Chung Chi College campus. 2006. Photo by Ho Ying

Ho Ying doing a tea service demonstration in her Hong Kong apartment. 2006. Photo by Emily Foster

While taking a look in the church, as people filed in for the Sunday afternoon service, Ho Ying and I spotted Man-On, a one-eyed orphan who Grandma had helped to raise at St. Christopher's. He worked at Chung Chi College, but was retiring that fall. When Ho Ying introduced me in Cantonese and explained who I was, I saw his one eye mist over as he eagerly shook my hand. Ho Ying took our picture in front of Granddad's chapel. I was disappointed to learn that St. Christopher's Baby Home had been torn down to make room for skyscraping apartments. St. Christopher's, however, still thrives today as a charitable organization that provides social services to those in need in Hong Kong. Although Grandma's Baby Home isn't around anymore, there are several St. Christopher's group homes for troubled youth throughout the city.

Ho Ying and I had lots of good talks about the Tonges. "Auntie Muriel was very kind to me, but I was a little scared of her at first. She was the first western person who ever really spoke to me."

When Ho Ying left her father's house to move in with the Tonges, she had wanted to share a room with A Kwan, rather than with my aunt Elizabeth. Eventually, though, as weeks passed over into months, Ho Ying learned to love the Tonges. "They were so friendly and kind to me. Your Grandma treated me like one of her own children. Your aunt Elizabeth and I became good friends. We played together all the time."

When the Tonges left Hong Kong for good, she'd cried into her pillow at night knowing how much she would miss them. On the other hand, she knew she wasn't ready to leave her father and her homeland. She and the Tonges remained in touch, and Grandma continued to help Ho Ying financially throughout her school years.

As a tribute to my Grandma's kindness over the years, Ho Ying now proudly sponsors three underprivileged children around Asia. "If it weren't for Auntie Muriel's help me over the years, I wouldn't be where I am today," Ho Ying told me earnestly. "I will never let myself forget."

Along with visiting sites that are significant on a personal level, I took in some of the famous attractions of Hong Kong, such as the jade market (where I had my first lesson in what would be a long course in bargaining), the vibrant nightlife of Victoria Harbour, the tourist-packed Peak Tram, as well as a solo expedition to see the 10, 000 Buddha's monastery, to name a few.

By the time my last night arrived, I felt ready for Yangshuo, where I would be teaching for the next six months. I was anxious to get going and unpack my bags in a new home. As much as I enjoyed seeing the places in Hong Kong I'd always heard about, I didn't think Hong Kong was the place for me. I'm not the type who indulges in urban chaos. Like most major cities, I found Hong Kong to be the kind of place that was about conquering nature, cutting down mountains and filling in harbours. Although I found it to be an interesting collision of cultures from the East and West, before long my senses were overwhelmed. On my last night in Hong Kong, I looked up to the little moon—pale and delicate—hovering over the neon spectacle. Though dim and distant, it was the one true light, and it comforted me. Though so much of Grandma's Hong Kong had been torn down, redesigned, and rebuilt, that quiet moon was still the same.

Soon I would be moving to Mainland China, chasing after more of Grandma's stories, and stories of my own. Although I would only be there for six months, I hoped to experience a taste of the affection my Grandma still feels for China. I couldn't wait to savour the food and smells, meet her people, and meet people of my own.

I knew it was going to be fantastic.

CPSIA information can be obtained at www.ICGtesting.com
Printed in the USA
LVOW08s0507160814

399377LV00002B/22/P

9 780595 529575